Critical Studies Series

WILLIAM FAULKNER:
The Yoknapatawpha Fiction

WILLIAM FAULKNER:
The Yoknapatawpha Fiction

edited by
A. Robert Lee

VISION PRESS · LONDON
ST. MARTIN'S PRESS · NEW YORK

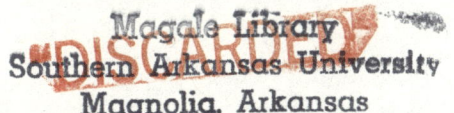

193200

Vision Press Ltd.
c/o Vine House Distribution
Waldenbury, North Common
Chailey, E. Sussex BN8 4DR

and

St. Martin's Press, Inc.
175 Fifth Avenue
New York
N.Y. 10010

ISBN (UK) 0 85478 465 9
ISBN (US) 0 312 03571 3

Library of Congress Cataloging-in-Publication Data

William Faulkner: the Yoknapatawpha fiction/edited by A. Robert Lee.
  (Critical studies series)
  ISBN 0-312-03571-3
  1. Faulkner, William, 1897–1962—Criticism and interpretation.
2. Yoknapatawpha County (imaginary place).
  I. Lee, A. Robert, 1941–   II. Series.
[PS3505.U97B4 1990]   89-48755
                                                                        CIP

A CIP catalogue record for this book is also available from the British Library.

© 1990 by Vision Press Ltd.
First published in the U.S.A. 1990

All rights reserved

Printed and bound in Great Britain by
Billing & Sons, Worcester.
Typeset by Galleon Photosetting,
Ipswich, Suffolk.
MCMLXXXX

Contents

		page
	Introduction by *A. Robert Lee*	7
1	Faulkner's Fortunate Geography by *James H. Justus*	19
2	Modernist Faulkner? A Yoknapatawpha Trilogy by *A. Robert Lee*	42
3	Faulkner, Women and Yoknapatawpha: From Symbol to Autonomy by *Faith Pullin*	64
4	Law, Justice and Justification in William Faulkner by *Eric Mottram*	85
5	Carnival Yoknapatawpha: Faulkner's *Light in August* by *David Timms*	128
6	Marking Out and Digging In: Language as Ritual in *Go Down, Moses* by *Graham Clarke*	147
7	The Snopes Trilogy by *Andrew Hook*	165
	Notes on Contributors	181
	Index	183

Introduction

by A. ROBERT LEE

> Loving all of it even while he had to hate some of it because he knows now that you don't love because: you love despite; not for the virtues, but despite the faults.
> —William Faulkner, 'Mississippi' (1954)

> Beginning with *Sartoris* I discovered that my own little postage stamp of native soil was worth writing about and that I would never live long enough to exhaust it, and that by sublimating the actual into the apocryphal I would have complete liberty to use whatever talent I might have to its absolute top. It opened up a gold mine of other people, I created a cosmos of my own. I can move these people around like God. . . .
> —Interview with Jean Stein, *Paris Review* (1956)

Whether, in truth, it is always a complex fate to be an American, it rarely can have been more so than in the case of William Faulkner (1897–1962). Born into a Mississippi, a South, where 'The War', that is The American Civil War (1861–65), and why it was fought and lost, still offered an everyday reference, he lived long enough down the century to find himself like other Southerners—white and black—implicated in all the processes of change brought on by the early Kennedy Presidency and its insistence on formal desegregation and Civil Rights. That, together with witnessing the South in the Depression and the slow decline of its agrarian economy, for a politically-minded descendant of Mississippi's first white settler clans might have been complexity enough. But Faulkner brought to bear further complicating energies. Despite his frequent disclaimers, and before all else, his would be a lifetime of literary craft, an unremitting output of stories, novels, essays and interviews which, though they occasionally deal in other themes, indeed in other places, return inexorably to Mississippi and the world of his birthright. For it fell to him, as quite none before or after, to transpose that 'actual' Mississippi into the 'apocryphal' kingdom he called Yoknapatawpha, of which with justice and not a little typical wryness he proclaimed himself 'Sole Owner & Proprietor'.

The huge canvas which makes up Yoknapatawpha, and which yields some of the best established American fiction of our time, unsurprisingly has been a source of debate and controversy. On the one hand, detractors thought him given beyond recall to Gothic extravagance, the creator of a Deep South unleavened by human reason or intimacy or love in any 'normal' sense. Was not Poe's 'The Fall of the House of Usher', with its fissured mansion, black tarn and brother-sister guilt, too evidently a sponsoring script for Faulkner's blighted dynasties, his dramas of baroque and violent emotion? Was not his own fiction, too, it was asked with genuine sobriety, born of the mentality which had produced Margaret Mitchell's *Gone with the Wind* (1936), both the bestseller and the ensuing Clark Gable-Vivien Leigh movie of 1939? Had he not, to compound his offences further, buried himself in an idiom too histrionic and word-laden ever to command a genuine following? Little wonder that he went largely unread through the 1930s·or that few of his books managed to stay long in print.

Those who read him differently, however, and few did so more creditably or prophetically than Malcolm Cowley in *The Portable Faulkner* (1946), saw in Yoknapatawpha an altogether more engaging order of creation. Here, as nowhere before, was a South triumphantly made over into a domain where tragedy and comedy lay strikingly intertwined, where a specific region's history could plausibly be used to mirror generic and larger issues, where the feel of Mississippi's red clay and its cycle of weather and crop lay inside Faulkner's very prose, and where the story-telling for all that it inherited an ancient body of history and myth had truly been pushed to new ends and new reaches of style. Did not Faulkner, too, call upon a humour, a shaping sense of irony, which freed him of routine charges of solemnity or mere portentousness? Nearly three decades on from his death, the controversies

Introduction

for sure continue, but the balance clearly has come to lie in Faulkner's favour.

How, then, does the story evolve? Born of two ancestral Mississippi families, the Falkners and Butlers (a printing error in his first published volume, *The Marble Faun* (1924), gave his name as Faulkner and he decided to retain the 'u'), Faulkner as a young man affected something of the dandy, a would-be aesthete in an intractably provincial Oxford and Lafayette County. So, at least, attested his great Oxford friend and early supporter, the lawyer Phil Stone. Faulkner, in fact, might well have been thought no more than a true heir to the slightly rakish cast of his family line. That, among others, includes his namesake and paternal great-grandfather, Colonel William C. Falkner, a duellist in his youth, a Civil War veteran, a railway-builder who wrote a novel, *The White Rose of Memphis*, and who died in 1889 by the gun of a business and political rival. It also includes his grandfather, Colonel John Falkner, who on losing control of the family bank took his money in a bucket to a rival institution (an episode reworked in *The Town* (1957), the second of the Snopes novels).

Whatever the family provenance, however, it was as a young versifier and reviewer that the quiet son of Murry and Maud Butler Falkner (his father, who at different times had worked on the family railway, then in the livery-stable and hardware businesses, ended up Secretary and Business Manager of the University of Mississippi), made his literary bow, the youngster who had told a teacher in boyhood 'I want to be a writer like my great-grandaddy.' The path, perhaps not entirely auspicious, had been embarked on which eventually would lead to the authorship of fifty or so poems, nearly eighty short stories, and seventeen full-length novels.

Faulkner frequently and with some ruefulness referred to himself as 'a failed poet', a judgement none too unfair. But the verse he published, first in the University magazine *The Mississippian* (he did a year's study, mainly of English literature and French and Spanish, at the university), then in *The Marble Faun* (1924) and, still later, in *A Green Bough* (1933), lays down useful pointers for the fiction to follow (none more so than his deeply *symboliste* and dionysian 'L'Après-Midi d'un Faune'). Motifs recur of quest, desire, stasis and change, and the conundrum of time, together with an imagery of gods and satyrs, which under different guises he would time and again re-deploy in his story-telling. Faulkner as neophyte literateur also shows through in his early book reviews, and not least in the acknowledgement of Swinburne as a key beginning influence. His habits of genuinely wide and repeated reading would stay with him throughout his lifetime.

Inevitably, there were some false or at least odd starts. He created, in fact, a series of his own strange interludes: in 1918 as a would-be R.A.F. officer in Canada (a source of conflicting myths and credentials), in 1921 as a bookstore clerk in New York where he had hoped to meet sympathetic editors and publishers, and in 1922–24 as a postmaster at the University of Mississippi. But the major literary turn in his early life came about when, in 1925, having moved from Oxford to New Orleans and linked up with Sherwood Anderson and his literary circle, he published a series of well-written journalistic pieces in the *Times-Picayune* and the *Double-Dealer*. These would reappear in several later incarnations, principally *Salmagundi* (1932), *Mirrors of Chartres Street* (1953) and *New Orleans Sketches* (1955), to which should be added his *Sherwood Anderson and other Famous Creoles* (1926), a joint production with the artist William Spratling with a Preface by Faulkner written in parody of Anderson's style, and *Mosquitoes* (1927), where in the figure of Dawson Fairchild he again subjected Sherwood Anderson to his not inconsiderable satiric powers. Anderson, in truth, both times comes out unfairly. For his example, and Faulkner's crucial reading of Joseph Conrad (*Heart of Darkness* especially) and the James Joyce of *Dubliners*, had almost everything to do with the Mississippian's becoming a writer of fiction. Not that Faulkner's first novel, *Soldier's Pay* (1926), gave grounds for undue optimism, a stilted psychodrama whose several plots jostle for pride of place and which tells the story of a scarred and despairing airman's return from World War I to his native Georgia. The move into Faulkner's true subject, however, was to emerge momentously three years

Introduction

later with the first of his Yoknapatawpha novels, *Sartoris* (1929).

'You're a country boy', Anderson had told Faulkner, 'all you know is that little patch up there in Mississippi where you started from. But that's all right too.' More salient words could not have been spoken. Faulkner's impulse to make art of life, fiction of history, now and as if unstoppably had found its truest expression in reworking the lore and stored-up memories of his upbringing. Small town and country Mississippi, race, fundamentalist Christianity, a stunning inwardness with the physicality of the land in all its changes and markings, and an ear for the ironies (and silences) of local speech, became subject to his own need to get them all transposed into a coherent imaginative meaning and pattern. Mississippi as an inheritance, a living archive, had drawn from Faulkner as perhaps nothing else could have the recognition of where lay his overwhelming subject. His task would be to inscribe the old (and ongoing) in the new, Oxford and Lafayette County, Mississippi, in the great narrative cycle he conceived of as Yoknapatawpha.

Sartoris, its span the years between the Civil War and World War I, offers an inaugurating account of Yoknapatawpha as foremost a place of dynasty. Lineage, the weight of the fathers on their sons, Faulkner typifies in the evolution of the Sartoris family from its founding name of Colonel John Sartoris through to Bayard Sartoris, the former a buccaneer Jefferson County railway-builder and founder and the latter a damaged returnee war veteran from Europe. Names like Snopes, Sutpen, Benbow and others, appear in supporting rôles, all members of Yoknapatawpha dynasties whose doings would take on depth and resonance in succeeding novels. *Sartoris* cannot in itself be thought other than an uncertain achievement, its characters over-determined and its plot too formulaic. But it puts in place, for the first time, the essential components of Yoknapatawpha: the press of a frontier, ante-bellum and Confederate past upon the present, a community of vying families and property and land interests in an area once the home of Chickasaw Indians, the slavery-haunted equations of white and black, and an authentic sense of rootedness and terrain—in all, Faulkner's mythical kingdom as a place literally geographic and yet carried also in the inward and anything but peaceable minds and blood of its people. If New England's writers, a Hawthorne, Emerson or Thoreau, had created a northern imagined world, so, and far more fully even than the Boston-born Poe or the Missouri-bred Twain, Faulkner had likewise established one for the South, one also, and not unreasonably, destined to invite comparison with those other imagined worlds created an ocean away by the likes of Charles Dickens and Thomas Hardy.

So launched, Faulkner put his creative powers to full use. Throughout the 1930s, and slightly less so thereafter, there appeared the work which would best secure his reputation, each Yoknapatawpha novel or story complete in itself yet also part of an unfolding and overall chronicle. This work, too, revealed more than some mere story-telling archivist; Faulkner showed his hand as a virtuoso in the ways of narrative form, on his own terms a modernist from the unlikeliest of quarters. *The Sound and the Fury* (1929) tells the decline of the Compson family in four interlocking modes: that of the idiot brother Benjy who has only his sense-data to register change; that of Quentin, Harvard undergraduate and the prisoner of an inherited and compulsive Southern rhetoric of 'honour'; that of Jason, the mean, sardonic, obverse of any classic Greek quester; and that of Dilsey (as given in Faulkner's own authorial voice), the black, mothering servant-woman whose spirituality offers a touchstone overall. *As I Lay Dying* (1930), with its funny-grotesque yet tragic journey of the Bundrens through water and fire to bury their dead matriarch, Addie Bundren, Faulkner constructs as almost literally a book of Yoknapatawpha voices, a round of interacting monologues. Written in a legendary six weeks while he was doing night-work, it exhibits a focus and economy not always granted him.

Sanctuary (1931), a Southern thriller of sorts with ingredients of bootlegging, murder and prostitution, on Faulkner's own admission was something of a cheap shot. Yet, ironically, it gave him his best commercial success to date, not altogether surprising given a cast which deals in sexual and criminal violence and includes the winsome Temple Drake,

Introduction

the Memphis gangster Popeye, and the lawyer Horace Benbow. The still deeper violence within Yoknapatawpha, at least as manifested in its racial phobias, emerges in *Light in August* (1932). Joe Christmas's mixed blood serves as the very index of a society hexed by doctrines of purity and 'niggerdom'; such, in turn, is the witness of his crazed, Bible-spouting grandfather Doc Hines, his Yankee-abolitionist lover Joanna Burden, his failed saviour Rev. Hightower, and his eventual storm-trooper assassin Percy Grimm. At a serene opposite travels the pregnant Lena Grove, ever in search of Lucas Burch (*aka* Joe Brown), her errant and non-marrying 'husband', and comically pursued by her truly love-smitten admirer Byron Bunch. Yoknapatawpha rarely offers fare in turn more cruel, more bucolic, or more wittily sardonic.

Absalom, Absalom! (1936) may well be Faulkner's most striking, and certainly most assured, story of dynasty. In Thomas Sutpen and his Grand Design to beget a family clan, a Sutpen's Hundred, Faulkner tells another key American fable of disastrous innocence, one which has led to well-taken and frequent comparisons with Scott Fitzgerald's *The Great Gatsby*. Sent to the back door of a Virginia mansion in his youth by a flunkied black butler, a stunning rebuff to his hill-bred sense of democracy, Sutpen vows to become an empire-builder, a patriarch. The arena, in due course, moves from Virginia to Haiti to New Orleans to Yoknapatawpha, the latter shared with the Coldfields and Compsons and others of the county's would-be gentry. Sutpen's ambition and intended 'house', however, founder as if by decree, and once more on account of the ancient bans of miscegenation and incest. In the name of the Southern code, and in particular the 'protection' of a sister, his own disavowed black son is murdered by his white son who then seemingly disappears. Sutpen's subsequent, and not uncomic, procreative efforts result only in daughters, and in a burnt-down mansion presided over by his one demented (and black) descendant, Jim Bond. A history told at rising pace in slivers of memory, letters, personal witness and reconstructions of Sutpen's early and Yoknapatawpha past by Quentin Compson and his Canadian room-mate Shreve McCannon in their freezing Harvard dormitory, *Absalom, Absalom!* orchestrates its story

William Faulkner: The Yoknapatawpha Fiction

quite exhilaratingly, on any standard quite one of Faulkner's most consequential novels.

Nor, for Faulkner did the '30s stop there. First, a major shift took place in his domestic life with his marriage in 1929 to Estelle Oldham Franklin and the birth of their much-loved daughter, Jill, in 1933. Outwardly the couple lived a respectable, Oxford-based life, but their mutual hard drinking also had begun, an affliction which would eventually prove ruinous to the health of both. Then, in 1931, *Sanctuary*, a bestseller on publication, was adapted for the screen (as 'The Story of Temple Drake'), a prelude to Faulkner's own frequent stays in Hollywood between 1936 and 1946 as a scriptwriter and adapter of his own fiction. Drink or no, too, the fiction continued to get written: *These Thirteen*, his first story-collection in 1932; *Doctor Martino and Other Stories* in 1934; *Pylon*, his deeply and intrusively Eliot-influenced parable of an air-circus family set in a barely disguised New Orleans, in 1935; *The Unvanquished*, a story-cycle delineating two generations of Sartorises which came under fire for its too nostalgia-tinted picture of a cavalier Old South, in 1938; and *The Wild Palms*, two intersecting novellas (the second is called *Old Man*), which in juxtaposing the parallel convict lives of an ex-doctor and a train-robber explore inner as well as outer incarceration, in 1939. A decade later, in 1948, he issued *Intruder in the Dust*, also to be made into a film, a drama about the near-lynching of the wrongly accused black elder Lucas Beauchamp as witnessed by Chick Mallison, which to many still seemed an apologia for the South's being slow to move on racial equality. But of ranking importance with any of these must be *The Hamlet* (1940), the first of the Snopes trilogy, which would reach completion with *The Town* (1957) and *The Mansion* (1959).

Snopesian Yoknapatawpha could not be a place less aristocratic, a South fallen from glory and given over to criminal stealth and cunning. The Snopeses operate as rodent humanity, a warren of predators pledged overwhelmingly to self-interest and the cash nexus. Begot respectively by Flem and Eula Snopes, he a rogue trader and eventual banker and she all country voluptuousness, their kin include in their roll-call different kinds of swindler (Flem himself and I. O. Snopes), a

Introduction

bank robber (Byron Snopes), a trafficker in pornography (the immortally named Montgomery Ward Snopes), a stud (Virgil Snopes), a pig-farmer (Orestes Snopes), an idiot youth who falls in love with a cow (Ike Snopes), and assorted others, like the malign child-minder Doris Snopes, or the two also parodically named Snopeses, the grocer Wallstreet Panic Snopes, and the carpenter Watkins Products Snopes. The Snopeses's different conspiracies and shenanigans Faulkner tells in the main through three highly different yet interlocking narrators, the lawyer Gavin Stevens, the sewing-machine salesman V. K. Ratcliff, and Ratcliff's nephew Chick Mallison. The consensus has for the most part favoured *The Hamlet,* not least because of its often brutally funny sense of human guile. But the trilogy deserves to be read as unified and continuous story-telling, if not without blemish a tribute to Faulkner's sheer inventive stamina.

Faulkner as short-story writer, too, needs separate recognition. Besides the collections already mentioned (*These Thirteen, Doctor Martino and Other Stories,* and *The Unvanquished*), the list includes *Go Down, Moses and Other Stories* (1942) which, complicatingly, Faulkner himself referred to as a novel, *Knight's Gambit* (1949) and, as a kind of *summa,* the *Collected Stories of William Faulkner* (1950). If, invidiously, one had to select a classic Yoknapatawpha half-dozen, they would in every likelihood include some or all of the following: 'A Rose For Emily' (1930), the story of a spinster who, behind the genteel façade of her family house, murders and then preserves the body of a lover who planned to leave her, for all its Gothic armature a vintage study of human loneliness; 'Red Leaves' (1930), one of Faulkner's classic Chickasaw stories which looks at the shared patrimony of the land, red, black and white; 'Dry September' (1931), a chilling description of a lynch drama with a wrongly accused black victim and Klan-style mob leader in which Faulkner locates the violence in terms of the land and climate; 'That Evening Sun' (1931), narrated by Quentin Compson, which depicts the likely impending murder of the Compson black houseservant Nancy Mannigoe by her husband Jesus in the face of the family's insouciance; 'Barn Burning' (1939), a Snopes episode in which Ab Snopes runs foul of the de Spain family,

William Faulkner: The Yoknapatawpha Fiction

a contest of wills between the landless and the propertied in ancestral Yoknapatawpha; and 'A Courtship' (1948), another of Faulkner's stories of as he called them 'The Old Days', the rivalry for the love of an Indian girl between the young Ikkemotubbe (later to become a Chickasaw patriarch) and the river-helmsman David Hogganback which ends in a mutual if uneasy respect. *Go Down, Moses,* seven tales in all, yields Faulkner's most Conradian story-telling, dense, iconic portraits of Yoknapatawpha's mixed Indian, white and black heritage told mainly through the young Ike McCaslin. Each McCaslin has to face the implication of the actions of the clan founder, Lucius Quintus Carothers McCaslin, as disclosed in the family ledgers, and nowhere more stirringly than in 'The Old People', 'The Bear', and the retrospective 'Delta Autumn'.

In some ways Faulkner's post-war years represented a decline, yet paradoxically they were to bring him his greatest honours. Foremost was the award of the Nobel Prize for Literature in 1950, the implication of which he made clear in his memorable acceptance speech:

> I feel this award was not made to me as a man, but to my work—a life's work in the agony and sweat of the human spirit, not for glory and least of all for profit, but to create out of the human spirit something that did not exist before.

Other awards followed in quick succession. In 1951 the French gave him a *Légion d'Honneur,* not a little because of the Maurice Coindreau and other translations of his work and the support of Albert Camus (which had also led to his play *Requiem for A Nun* (1951), with its reintroduction of Temple Drake and Deep South murder-plot, being performed as much in France as America). In 1955 came the National Book Award for Fiction, and in its train later the same year the Pulitzer Prize for the highly stylized *A Fable* (1954), Faulkner's own anthem for doomed youth set in World War I France. For the State Department he made visits to Brazil in 1954, Nagano, Japan, in 1955, and Greece in 1957, none of which inhibited his public condemnations of Franco's Spain, McCarthyism, and the abuse of black Southerners. The latter, however, brought controversy upon him. Why,

Introduction

against his own often repeated argument, should the South be allowed to make its own adjustments and changes, free of 'liberal' Northern interference, when so signally it had failed to do previously? From 1957–62, he became Writer-in-Residence at the University of Virginia (he courteously referred to Virginia as 'The Mother of the South'), which produced his extraordinary run of classroom interviews. Their sustained and highly detailed show of memory, for a man often close to alcoholic collapse, offer their own kind of memorial. Alongside *A Fable* and *The Mansion*, there remained *The Reivers* (1962), 'A Reminiscence' as Faulkner called it, the charming, picaresque story of 11-year Lucius Priest's visit in the company of Boon Hogganbeck first to Miss Reba's brothel in Memphis and then the racetrack in the town of Parsham. Whatever else, Faulkner's wit had in no way lessened. It helped, too, assuage for others the ending of his life in a heart-attack in Oxford in July 1962.

Faulkner, and Yoknapatawpha, have cast a long shadow. The influence extends through several generations of Southern writers, from Robert Penn Warren to William Styron, from Eudora Welty and Flannery O'Connor to Carson McCullers and Shirley Ann Grau, and of Afro-American tradition, from Richard Wright and Ralph Ellison to Ernest Gaines. Almost any discussion of 'The Mind of the South', be the issue history, race, religion or terrain, requires a reference to his work. In like manner, Faulkner as a literary innovator, a maker of narrative for whom Yoknapatawpha supplies only the occasion, has to be acknowledged. Rarely can so past-minded a writer have attempted so modern or modernist a repertoire of story-telling styles. None of which is to exempt the flaws in his work, the wrong turnings, or to step around the fact that for a certain kind of readership Faulkner simply fails to attract. But it does help explain the proliferation of biographies and critical studies, a continuing and by no means unfair or unexpected phenomenon given the general view of his achievement.

So, at least, also runs the assumption behind the present collection of essays. The four opening contributions come at Faulkner and his creation of Yoknapatawpha from a broad prospectus. James H. Justus tackles 'geography' in Faulkner as feeling and memory as well as literal place. My own essay pursues a seeming contradiction in Faulkner, one already alluded to, that of the author of *The Sound and the Fury*, *As I Lay Dying*, and *Absalom, Absalom!* as at once a giver of ancient writ and a modernist. The suggestion is offered that, cannily and intriguingly, he contrived to be both. Faith Pullin analyses issues of gender and matriarchy in the Yoknapatawpha texts, especially as expressed in figures like Caddy Compson, Addie Bundren, Joanna Burden, Temple Drake, and the inescapable black presence of Dilsey. Eric Mottram, in a broad-ranging essay which also makes use of *A Fable*, delineates the pivotal image of 'law' in Faulkner's Yoknapatawpha world, 'law' both as a system of control and an implied larger metaphysic.

The other three essays address specific Yoknapatawpha novels. David Timms subjects *Light in August* to Bakhtinian rules, the Joe Christmas-Lena Grove story in all its despair and hope as essentially a 'carnival' drama. Graham Clarke sees in *Go Down, Moses* a story-sequence, a novel, which enacts in the very prose upon the page Mississippi's weight as a place of heat, delta and wilderness. Finally, Andrew Hook re-evaluates the Snopes trilogy, a Yoknapatawpha under siege by a new and unrelentingly avaricious dispensation. However different their emphasis, these essays proceed from a shared and undiminishing sense of Faulkner's importance, and of Yoknapatawpha as one of the indelible landscapes of modern fiction.

1
Faulkner's Fortunate Geography

by JAMES H. JUSTUS

1

For more than four decades two related assumptions have punctuated much of the commentary on Faulkner and his sense of place: that his descriptive accuracy and detail derived from his filio-pietism and self-conscious regionalism; and that, despite the author's intimacy with his geography, Yoknapatawpha is a triumph of creative self-sufficiency, the product of an aesthetic imagination whose authority is irrelevant to its cartographic models, Oxford and Lafayette County, Mississippi. The lurking contradictions in these two assumptions, beginning with Malcolm Cowley's chronological reconstruction in 1946 and continuing with most of the critical formalists, have not been resolved so much as they have simply been absorbed in the newer psycho-biographical approaches to Faulkner. Indeed, only in recent years have we become aware of the intensity of Faulkner's relationship to both family and place, but that complexity should never distract us from the author's own highest priority: his art.[1]

Jeremy Hooker has observed that place is one of those facts that can actually 'inhibit the poet's sense of movement, and allow the dust of familiarity to settle on all things'.[2] Faulkner never allowed this to happen because his first loyalty was to his art, not place and not family. I am arguing here that only an extravagant valuation of art could transmute the author's ambivalent family relations and the happy availability of familiar, but inert, setting into the kinetic proliferation of the most impressive body of American fiction in this century.

2

As his letters indicate, Faulkner was always happy to return from Hollywood to Mississippi, where he could play Old Maid, eat watermelon, and watch it rain, especially when he had brought back 'enough jack' to repair the house. After winning the Nobel Prize, he thought of Oxford as a refuge as well as a home; in one letter he declares, 'I have deliberately buried myself in this little lost almost illiterate town, to keep out of the way so that news people won't notice and remember me.' While there is no disputing Faulkner's love of his postage stamp of native soil, critics have made more of a fetish of it than the author himself ever did. After 1950 he dreaded the invasion of his privacy, but for most of his career he was eager enough to see, talk with, and entertain out-of-towners—for example, Harrison Smith, to whom he thanks in 1935 for bringing a 'suave metropolitan breath' into his 'bucolic midst'.[3] The Blotner biography first revealed the fact that for all the homebody stories that the novelist himself encouraged, Faulkner spent a surprising amount of time, and not always reluctantly, *away* from Oxford—and considerably more than that in the hankering to get away. By the time of his death his plans for a permanent home in Charlottesville, Virginia, had progressed far beyond the speculative stage.

The birth of Yoknapatawpha is by now a familiar story, but the dynamics of its nurturance less so. Like an architect or planner, Faulkner undertook his task first as the *possession* of place—accepting what was behind his life and before his eyes—and then, second, as the *creation* of place—making a pre-existent actuality conform to his abstract mapping. Faulkner's emotional experience of Oxford included what one social geographer calls the 'drudgery of place', the sense of being inexorably bounded by the established 'scenes and symbols and routines' of home.[4] But if he sometimes

Faulkner's Fortunate Geography

betrayed frustration with Oxford—its aggressive anti-aestheticism, its restrictive social divisions and pretensions, its burdensome cultus of honour within which complacent family members showed little disposition to be grateful—his town, partly because of these very shortcomings, offered itself richly for aesthetic shaping. Once, when invited to write a non-fiction book on the Mississippi River, Faulkner responded: 'I dont believe I can do it. I am a novelist, you see: people first, where second.'[5]

People first, where second: though, as I shall argue, even this statement of priorities does not in the final view summarize Faulkner's achievement, it fairly describes his compositional habits. In his abstracts of projected works for publishers he makes nothing significant of his Oxford-Jefferson settings; they invariably focus on characters and their interactions. In concentrated periods of composition he sometimes forgot stories he had dispatched to his agent; a 1940 note to Harold Ober, who had inquired of a rewritten version of 'Rose of Lebanon', is revealing generally: 'could you name a character or so, then I will remember it.' In 1946, when he wrote Ober praising Malcolm Cowley's job of 'Spoonrivering my apocryphal county', the term suggests a work comprised of smaller pieces assembled so as to evoke a larger community as matrix, but it is also a reminder that Edgar Lee Masters' technique was to emphasize the persons of *Spoon River* rather than geography. Indeed, even Faulkner's notion of character differs slightly from his actual creation of characters; his direction, at least at the conceptualizing stage, was not from the particular to the general, from Oxford to the world, but the reverse. He saw himself tapping into no local reservoir for his art, but the deeper one used by precursors throughout western culture. As he wrote to Cowley, 'Art is simpler than people think because there is so little to write about. All the moving things are eternal in man's history and have been written before.' About the ambitious novel that would finally be published simply as *A Fable*, Faulkner wrote thus to R. K. Haas at Random House, 'If the book can be accepted as a fable, which it is to me, the locale and contents wont matter.'[6]

For readers as well as booksellers, locale and contents of course do matter, but for Faulkner their de-emphasis was the logical consequence of his aesthetic principles. As Robert Lowell once observed of Faulkner, 'his by-path, Mississippi, was no by-path, but a universe.'[7] Though it is most pronounced in the works of the 1950s, Faulkner's tendency to equate literary art with ancient patterns, grand abstractions and universal themes was lodged in his consciousness from the beginning and accounts in part for the bewildering recurrence in the early writing of knights and enchanted landscapes. For all its promiscuous ancestry (Pre-Raphaelite medievalism, *Jurgen*, Beardsley, John Held, Jr., *The Yellow Book*, the Decadent poets), place in the apprentice work is fully conceived. But its marmoreal solidity, fixed by repetitive urns, marble colonnades, and enclosed gardens, defeats whatever vitality can be mustered by its dryads, questing idealists and allegorical wraiths. Faulkner liked limits, as the boundaries of his Yoknapatawpha maps suggest, but he also liked to trespass beyond the stability and circumscription of place. The worlds of Pierrot and Sir Galwyn, even the forests especially grown for knightly quests, were too limited for his trespassing imagination.

A critic once remarked that Faulkner was 'fortunate in his geography'.[8] As his own maps suggest, the fictional Yoknapatawpha features the same range of diverse soils and topographies as Lafayette County: a stretch of northern Mississippi that can reasonably comprise the Yazoo-Mississippi Delta, the brown loam region known as the Black Belt, the sand clay hills, the flatwoods, and the prairie, and a northeast hill country, as well as a river called on older maps Yockony Patawfa. Faulkner's conception of this boundaried county—perhaps as early as 1924—preceded its piecemeal articulation. The first map, appended to *Absalom, Absalom!* in 1936 establishes his sense of coherence, and, with further modifications in the map for Cowley's *Portable Faulkner* ten years later, Yoknapatawpha is stabilized. But as one critic has observed, the aesthetic need for coherence and stability is always countered by an even greater impulse—to close boundaries, to revise former signs of closure, to add more and take away nothing. Faulkner's characteristic energy, out of a reluctance to complete his own design, is to reconstitute 'new designs out of old ones'.[9]

Faulkner's Fortunate Geography

Faulkner's chorography, like any map-making, was an exercise for abstracting pre-existent creation; it allowed this writer to take a long and high view of his demesne, bordered and encompassed, but he required more than cardinal points and natural features.[10] Being unable to humanize his world on one page—which would have meant superimposing prior narratives upon cartography itself, a self-defeating if not impossible act—Faulkner did the next best thing: he stripped his prior narratives of all enveloping and interlocking texture until they stood as iconography, signs and scenes of meaningful human enterprise. For Faulkner sites become memorable not because, as in folklore, the communal mind remembers and transmits the events associated with them, but because Faulkner himself, as 'sole proprietor' of his world, remembers and transmits the association. A grand site, such as the courthouse, may have multiform appearances, but it attains significance because it is 'where Temple Drake testified'; and the Confederate monument in the square, though its presence is logged in work after work, is important as place because it is the landmark 'which Benjy had to pass on his *left* side'. But Faulkner's terrain and its radiated meaning includes the humble, too: the bridge at Frenchmen's Bend 'which washed away so Anse Bundren and his sons could not cross it with Addie's body' or the saw mill 'where Byron Bunch first saw Lena Grove'. We have no textual evidence that Yoknapatawphans remember the courthouse, the monument, the bridge, or the saw mill for the reasons that Faulkner designates. The sites of his world iconographically ratify his power as creator.

This tack is probably Faulkner's most familiar technique in his depiction of place—attributing the specialness of particular sites to what happened there. But what about the prior narratives themselves, the referents without which the map rubrics would remain arcane? Following the Faulknerian formula—*people first, where second*—we customarily think of the author's extensive gallery of characters as the propelling energy in the works, that a Snopes or a Compson make their places significant because of who they are and what they do. Since intensity and recapitulation—and sometimes ubiquity—characterize the presence and influence of such figures as some of the Snopeses, Joe Christmas, Lena Grove, Jason Compson, Addie Bundren and many others, the environment in which their compulsions are enacted absorbs and radiates back those compelling, extravagant aspects of character. Directing that process, however, is neither character nor narrative, but style. If the rubrics on the maps are stripped-down versions of narrative, the novels are so narratively full-blown, so excessive in their interlockings, that they in effect become narrative versions of rhetoric.

3

We may in our affective response 'believe' in Faulknerian setting; after all, the tangible detail in credible contexts, the key to realistic scene-painting, is common in the Yoknapatawpha works. But the sweep of the creator's vision is so grand it requires as *priority* an idiom for projecting that world; it is an idiom that while it happily detaches itself from the static derivativeness of the apprentice writing, constructs place that answers more to the writer's internal aesthetic need than to geographical realism. Yoknapatawpha is primarily a geography of unreality stylistically fashioned as a place to which individuals must adjust themselves and their rhythms. Unlike New Valois, the Gulf Shore, France, and other settings in the non-Yoknapatawpha works, Faulkner's county is depicted as ancient, resistless, a quietly shaping force to which human will must submit. We like to think that the rhythms of Lena Grove are consonant with, perhaps even the human equivalent of, the natural landscape in which she is a transient, while those of Joe Christmas are the tragic resistant counterforce to the place he circularly travels. But both are the subjects of a Calvinist creator completing *his* imaginative schema, not theirs; these migratory pilgrims momentarily recreate the place they pass through even as they are recreated momentarily by it, but both submitter and resister, passivist and activist, fulfil their rôles within a world preshaped by Faulkner and his vision. Undergraduates sometimes conclude that the Bundrens are at one with their environment. This formula, if not the romantic sentiment it tries to affirm, is bleakly true. *As I Lay Dying* reads as if Faulkner had set out to show how animal and human, materiality and phenomenology, animate and inanimate are all reversible categories that rain, flood and fire only exacerbate. As in early expressionistic films, the road appears, unspools, disappears beneath the mules' pace; the solidity of the Bundren house dissolves into optical and ocular angles and channels; measurements, sizes, geometric shapes and precision of detail are insistently referred to only to be subjected to risible irrelevance, just as the logic of Cash's carpentry collapses into nonsense. The 'one trouble with this country', says Dr. Peabody, is how it 'hangs on too long', creating its inhabitants 'in its implacable and brooding image'. But the country hangs on too long because Faulkner, here a down-home surrealist, would have it so.[11]

A simpler device, magnitude—in which one constituent element of landscape is simply isolated from and elevated beyond its context—is most conspicuous in the Tall Convict's story in *The Wild Palms*. By all accounts, Faulkner's flooded Mississippi is only barely related to the actual historic event of 1937. This story required the kind of scene in which sky and surface are melded indistinguishably together and ordinary energies of a river current are hiked perceptibly into furious motion indifferent to puny human control. Within this primordial chaos Faulkner hovers over his deep, creating first the symbolic human family and then situating it within a tribal economy; in the undifferentiated space of liquid and light, the island and the Cajun's levee assume importance almost as ur-place.

Like old world sites for certain European writers, locality for Faulkner is rich in history, oppressively so. Yet the burden of local landscape, like the burden of the past, is less oppressive in its shaping determinism because it is assumed as an aesthetic act. Elizabeth Bowen once wrote that in return for the inspiration of one's environment, which supplies atmosphere, texture and flavour, the writer owes 'pieties' to the enclave that gave birth to him and his creation. That kind of debt would seem to apply less to Faulkner than, say, to his fellow writer and friend from Oxford, Stark Young, for whom the appurtenances and values of place as well as the ancestors who possessed them were claustrophobically preserved. The kind of emotional subservience to the locale that we find in *So Red the Rose* is Young's repayment for its inspiration, but its mode—essayistic, idealized transcriptions—is the untransformed tribute; Faulkner's repayment for inspiration is creation, not even recreation, and his mode is melodramatic, theatrical: the reciprocated gesture of something new, not something preserved. To 'love a land means to look for transfigurations', says the poet John Riley[12]—which is what we see happening to northern Mississippi as Yoknapatawpha emerges over the course of Faulkner's career. Moving 'people around like God' was the novelist's prerogative, Faulkner once asserted; and in an important way the novelist also had to provide his own proprietary space within which they could be so moved.

Faulkner probably realized that he was fortunate in his geography, but being so was clearly not satisfying to his ambition. If the distinctive quadrants of his maps, each devised as appropriate setting for distinctive human acts, answered to the demands of artifice, so too did those places in his narratives. Like the map-making, Faulkner's style is the assertion of the creator, the assertion of his being, his identity—not those of his characters. That signature discourse is unashamedly rhetorical, the window of a sensibility that wants to incorporate everything into itself. Articulating this drive toward inclusiveness is a style so accretive—repetitive words and phrases that like musical variations evolve, nuance by nuance, into different planes of significance—that language itself is the privileged component in Faulkner's art. The discovery of 'the way it was' for Faulkner involved the absorption of geography into his sensibility, which then tested the amenability of place to its inherent potentialities, continuities, and even its unresolvable extrapolations. The impulse required a rhetoric of magnification, at times a nose-thumbing irreality so radical that his style often seems to be positing only itself. For Faulkner the redundant, the extravagant, the hyperbolic are reified into a way of seeing.

Faulkner's Fortunate Geography

If, as some critics believe, Faulkner modelled his unhurried, digressive, parenthetical sentence structure on the tale-swapping flow of courthouse characters, it is unlikely that he found on benches or in country stores any live models for his diction and imagery. Only the self-conscious aspirant to high literary art could transform the rural lore of his time and place by the linguistic mannerisms so inimical to it—by idioms that exist only in books. Faulkner relishes the chance to invest the people and places of his ordinary world with attributes out of myth, legend, literature and popular culture: Gavin Stevens as Don Quixote; Sutpen as Faustus, Beelzebub, King David; Flem Snopes as Satanic usurper; Byron, Lena, and newborn son as perambulating Holy Family; Ike Snopes as medieval knight; Miss Reba's brothel as boarding-house; the Varner schoolhouse as the grove of Dionysius. Further, his reserve of embellishing and enhancing tricks is expended not only on the rites generally accorded significance (courtship and adultery customs, weddings and funerals), but also on the vast range of human interaction from the trivial to the symbolic (trades, merchandise sales, bartered exchanges; card games; dog-breeding; grudges, fights, country mayhem). And further: the aggrandizing mode, Faulkner's version of Milton's 'answerable style', is committed not merely to works of appropriate matter (*Absalom, Absalom!*); it freely informs the mock-heroic and the merely comic (*The Hamlet, The Reivers*) and those works that mingle the serious and the comic (*The Sound and the Fury, Light in August*). It even has its political version in the rodomontade of Gavin Stevens (*Intruder in the Dust, The Town*).

We sometimes assume, for all our professed high appraisals of art, that aesthetic versions of geography are merely evocations of prior actuality—that is, George Caleb Bingham's canvases of Mississippi boatmen and Washington Irving's verbal transcriptions of the Hudson Valley must necessarily be weak imprints of the real things. But in evoking a place the artist also creates it, not only because senses distort and memory selects, but also because the pride of human making asserts its primacy: shaping, not reshaping, is a self-sufficient activity. The vitality of Yoknapatawpha stems from something far more crucial than the simple intersection of memory and imagination. Gaston Bachelard has observed that 'often when we think we are describing we merely imagine.'[13] From what I can determine, Faulkner never fooled himself that he was only describing, but he would not have liked that dismissive 'merely imagine'. He attributed both reality and value to his determination to let art make amends for defective actuality. This substitutionary motive he refers to several times: having to 'invent a world a little different from the shabby one' we all inhabit.[14] But if we tend to overvalue Faulkner's sense of place, it is because we can never quite believe that art can supersede even a shabby nature. 'Space is transformed into place as it acquires definition and meaning', writes geographer Yi-Fu Tuan; in the case of Faulkner's county, that place was purely private until it was defined by art, which, as this writer's work demonstrates, has its own elisions of suppression and substitution.[15]

4

Daniel Aaron is probably right when he asserts that Faulkner is 'most Southern when he is concentratingly local'—that is, when he describes harness shops or discusses the personalities of hound dogs. And Robert Penn Warren long ago in a review of *These Thirteen* made a valid point when he thought he detected less 'stylization' in the works that are 'intimately related to their locality'.[16] But Faulkner is the most singular when he is so local that the harness shop or hound becomes something else through the sheer pressure of imaginative concentration; and the specifics of his locale, even in Yoknapatawpha, are transformed into something else by a linguistic heightening that can only be called stylization.

It is now a little startling to read the preface that Phil Stone kindly wrote for Faulkner's first volume. One wonders where among the mannered landscapes out of Swinburne and Beardsley he found 'a man steeped in the soil of his native land'. And if the pages of *The Marble Faun* fail to ratify Stone's promise of the sunlight and blue hills of northern Mississippi, we also wonder about Faulkner's native inspiration as late

Faulkner's Fortunate Geography

as 1926 in *Mayday*, in which Sir Galwyn, accoutred with a sword, also sports 'morion and hausberk and greaves'.[17] The fact is that Faulkner was first an aesthete and then a modernist before he became a regionalist; and even after he began exploring the possibilities of his Yoknapatawpha he never sacrificed his first two identities. His flourishes of seignorial pride are all gestures toward his made place, not his found place.

There may be something more personal than the rôles of either aesthete or modernist in his persistent fondness for 'Carcassonne'—a piece of almost pure setting, the site for narrative situation rather than narrative and for meditation rather than action. In his seaport garret, amid the 'fairy patterings' and 'whispering arpeggios' of rats around his tar-paper bed, the young narrator-artist cries out:

> *I want to perform something bold and tragical and austere ... me on a buckskin pony with eyes like blue electricity and a mane like tangled fire, galloping up the hill and right off into the high heaven of the world.*[18]

The fiery steed is surely the artist's imagination, the gift of difference in a place of deprivation.

A canny alternative to this symbolic, abstract soaring is the little digression on the mule in *Flags in the Dust*, in which the *context* of discourse is aggressively vernacular while the *plane* of discourse is self-consciously oracular. The setting is the countryside (not yet named Yoknapatawpha) where Bayard and Narcissa drive among the Sartoris tenants, one of whom operates a molasses-making mill; but the mule, plodding its monotonous circle among the cane-pith, is not depicted from any of these characters' perspectives. 'Some Homer of the cotton fields should sing the saga of the mule and his place in the South', it begins, and as his own home-grown Homer, the author sings in something like 350 words the natural history of an unnatural animal whose domestic service to its owners is a mixture of meek servitude and stubborn resistance. The passage is a triumph of elevated diction and rhetorical periodicity, occasionally broken by mundane, nodding asides. The mock splendor of the paean closes on a note of mortality and continuity:

William Faulkner: The Yoknapatawpha Fiction

Alive, he is haled through the world, an object of general derision; unwept, unhonored and unsung, he bleaches his awkward accusing bones among rusting cans and broken crockery and worn-out automobile tires on lonely hillsides while his flesh soars unawares against the blue in the craws of buzzards.[19]

Both the buckskin pony and the mule serve as Faulkner's Pegasus carrying the author as stylist, the function that he most nourished throughout his career, whether as aesthete, modernist, or regionalist. The protagonist in *Mayday* experiences a godlike ecstasy as

a falling star, consuming the whole world in a single long swooping rush through measureless regions of horror and delight down down, leaving behind him no change of light nor any sound.[20]

The knight's transfiguring direction is different from that in 'Carcassonne', but, experimenting with syntax, by 1926 Faulkner has already seized upon his gift for the rhetorical heightening of unpromising subject-matter. Falling or soaring has less to do with Sir Galwyn or Mississippi mules than with the aesthetic vision of an author who never lost his impulse toward verbal intensification, even self-indulgence.

One textual signal of how the earthbound artist resists the restraint of humble detail, understatement and unencumbered narration is the frequency with which Faulkner seeks out the privileged terrain as an all-encompassing perspective for the possessing eye. Despite the absence of mountains in Yoknapatawpha, Faulkner transforms its actual hills into literary topography, sites especially composed for heightened vistas, from which he fashions what the eighteenth-century poets called 'prospects'. Higher ground invites rhetorical aggrandizement; ocular mastery means aesthetic and spiritual possession of the landscape. In *The Town* that higher ground begins as a nod toward realistic landscape:

There is a ridge; you drive on beyond Seminary Hill and in time you come upon it: a mild unhurried farm road presently mounting to cross the ridge and on to join the main highway leading from Jefferson to the world. And now, looking back and down, you see all Yoknapatawpha in the dying last of day beneath you.

Faulkner's Fortunate Geography

Fortunate geography is literally and literarily elevated:

> And you stand suzerain and solitary above the whole sum of your life beneath that incessant ephemeral spangling [of fireflies]. First is Jefferson, the center, radiating weakly its puny glow into space; beyond it, enclosing it, spreads the County, tied by the diverging roads to that center as is the rim to the hub by its spokes, yourself detached as God Himself for this moment above the cradle of your nativity and of the men and women who made you, the record and chronicle of your native land proffered for your perusal in ring by concentric ring like the ripples on living water above the dreamless slumber of your past; you to preside unanguished and immune above this miniature of man's passions and hopes and disasters. . . .[21]

Even the highest ridge in Yoknapatawpha is an unlikely promontory for any literal prospect, and a realistic topography, once it has served its narrative purpose, is quickly supplanted by an elevation and an unobstructed panorama that owe more to the epic than to the novel. Though the passage seems to resemble Bowen's theory of 'repayment' in which the writer pays homage to his native sacred place, it is invoked in the language of mastery, of ownership; and now, as if in appreciative response to the post-Cowley consensus of readers: *County* capitalized. Following this symbolic placement of the creator who surveys his own creation—the very image of the writer as self-celebrant—comes a miniature condensation of Faulkner's world: a roll-call of familiar names, Issetibbeha, Sutpen, Sartoris, McCallum, Varner, Snopes—Indians, planters, hillmen, rich and poor—'supine beneath you, stratified and superposed, osseous and durable with the frail dust and the phantoms. . .'. In linking the conventional notion of the frail dust of the dead with the living characters in his books, Faulkner in effect attributes permanence to his creation. Moreover, while the requisite pieties of place are embedded in the prospect, Faulkner's primary celebration, as the passage develops, is finally not Jefferson or Yoknapatawpha, but the human spirit that affirms light: the paean to a cultural abstraction calls forth a resolutely literary diction.

Another kind of stylistic self-consciousness occurs in a

similar passage in *Intruder in the Dust* in which the hieratic, incantatory prose for asserting identity and ownership is put to the service of regional defence. As Chick Mallison accompanies his uncle, Gavin Stevens, on an automobile ride into the heart of Beat Four in the Yoknapatawpha hills, an imaginary prospect begins, like that in *The Town*, realistically enough, with the vehicle straining in second gear up 'the main ridge', 'up and onto the last crest'; then 'he seemed to see his whole native land, his home . . . unfolding beneath him like a map in one slow soundless explosion.' In its two-and-a-half pages Faulkner asserts through Chick the honour of being shaped according to 'specific passions and hopes and convictions and ways of thinking and acting of a specific kind and even race', but because the assertion is hedged by threats from beyond the home, the passage is fraught with indecision and hurt. The vision of home—'the dirt, the earth' surveyed and reaffirmed by the eye—is forcibly joined to a larger vision beyond, through geography stretching to 'ultimate headlands', the 'waste of two oceans', and the Canadian 'barrier'. This geography beyond Yoknapatawpha is the north as enemy: 'not north but North, outland and circumscribing and not even a geographical place, but an emotional idea. . .'.[22] What confronts Chick is a 'curving semicircular wall' from which 'there looked down upon him . . . massed uncountable faces looking down at him and his in fading amazement and outrage and frustration', and the vision of comfortable regional identification thus turns into a kind of cultural shunning ceremony, one in which the spatial planes (*wall; looking down on*) are themselves agents of moral judgement. The passage resonates with Faulkner's own troubled feelings and commitments in this early stage of the Civil Rights struggle, and by 1954, the year of the *Brown v. Board of Education* decision, Faulkner would write of his home: 'you dont love because: you love despite; not for the virtues, but despite the faults.'[23]

This passage is a deflationary use of the device that Faulkner had already used with such effect in *Absalom, Absalom!* Whereas from the eminence of a Beat Four ridge Chick has his vision of hostility and alienation, Quentin and Shreve are unified and fused from the author's imaginary perspective in space, an epic device by which geography is made submissive to voracious human need and time is made momentarily subservient to human imagination. Even more than the privileged terrain, such enlarged and extended perspectives, because they stretch the ordinary narrative function of authorial control, invite stylistic inflation. Faulkner thus grandly eradicates distinctions between Shreve and Quentin not only as narrating intelligences, but also as individuals, a temporary state attributable to the intensity of their empathy with the Sutpen sons. This remarkable authorial move occurs in an incantatory swirl out of which comes now fusion, now metathasis, now New Orleans, now Cambridge, now 1860, now 1910. Faulkner's manipulation of characters-storytellers-fantasists is rhetorical, which is to say that the boldness is less a response to the demands of characterization or narrative than it is to the more general aesthetic needs of the author. The 'vaporizing breath' of Quentin-Shreve is itself the creator's surrogatory medium that summons up the 'shades' and 'shadows' of the recreating past. Moreover, the Poesque atmospheric layering here in Chapter 8 is anticipated in the previous chapter, in which Faulkner as mesmerist erases the differences between the two room-mates who, though 'born a continent apart', are connected 'in a sort of geographical transubstantiation by that Continental Trough', the great river that is not only a 'geologic umbilical', but is 'very Environment itself which laughs at degrees of latitude and temperature'. Faulkner's metaphoric excess is not a gratuitous paean to his storytellers' birthplaces (or even their extension, in the transubstantiated land from Mississippi to Alberta); it makes setting itself fantastic, the better to accommodate a gothic reprise, a tale better than *Ben-Hur*, in which the 'violent and unratiocinative djinns and demons' fill up and overflow the 'snug monastic coign' where they are generated.[24] The seance-like language renders interior and exterior settings interchangeable, just as it fuses and metathasizes characters. The source of both is the master of the djinns, the artist-medium.

5

With his happy indifference to genre, Faulkner exercises his aesthetic dominance over geography independent of his fiction. The recalcitrance of history and fact is as easily conquered by style as are character and narrative in the fiction. What would appear to be an appropriate piece for a travel magazine, 'Mississippi' disabuses the reader in the first paragraph by introducing 'the boy', a device that allows Faulkner maximum freedom to mingle memoir, description, historical information, geographical facts, and episodes of narrative. This semi-autobiographical point of view imposes a structure of feeling upon a discursive foray into guidebook writing. Here, too, in yet another roll-call, his fictional people (Sartoris, De Spain, Compson, McCaslin) are juxtaposed against historical battles (Manassas, Sharpsburg, Shiloh, Chickamauga). James B. Meriwether asks of such involvement, is the author 'making himself into a part of his fiction, or bringing his fiction into his own life?'[25] As his interviews and the biography suggest, Faulkner could reconstitute the self as easily as he could history and geography if doing so might contribute to the permanence of his art.

And if 'Mississippi' must have been a curious performance for the customary reader of *Holiday* in 1954, so too the regular reader of *Sports Illustrated* when he came upon 'Kentucky: May: Saturday' the following year. Ostensibly an account of the Kentucky Derby, it at one point duplicates the sightline of the spectator in the immediacy of the moment (horses once eight feet tall and ten feet long now become 'arrows twice that length and less than half that thickness'). But this bravura piece is notable for what Faulkner does with the sense of place not his own, a brilliant exercise in which he submits public images, clichés and stereotypes to his own stylistic fancies. The commissioned essay begins not with horses and riders, but with 'This saw Boone:' as historical prologue.[26] A disquieting syntactical inversion, the natural emphasis falls on the first word, making the relative pronoun more important than it would be in normal placement, but also requiring completion to make it meaningful. The particularized locale seen by the pioneer is re-envisioned by the writer in a verbal act that transfers the original act of exploration to this later articulator, the literary explorer who here puts his claim on Kentucky. A sentence whose very structure we would expect to elevate Boone instead elevates Faulkner. The strained linguistic order calls attention to, even while it assimilates, the archaic heroism of Boone's historic and literal exploration into the writer's own imaginative one.

Moreover, this quiet revisionism is earned by what is particularized in the rest of the paragraph. The sequence of settlement (the prodigal landscape is succeeded by the 'wild men' both red and white, who then name the villages) ends with 'Kentucky: the dark and bloody ground'; the economical paragraph encapsulates the familiar and popular images of the state by heavy emphasis on substantives whose very sounds are linked to Kentucky: Boone, gaps, salt licks, limestone springs, bourbon, all of which resonate in the public ear. That is, the passage cites the requisite images, themselves mundane through cultural overuse, and they are succeeded in the rest of the segment by two names—Lincoln and Stephen Foster—that carry even a greater burden of familiarity. All this as an introduction that in turn rivals Boone, salt licks, bourbon, or Lincoln as chief totemic symbol for contemporary Kentucky. In this piece of cultural journalism Faulkner uses style, simultaneously his tool and weapon, to forge an artifact that defamiliarizes its familiar subject while drawing attention to the creator who wields that tool and weapon.

6

David Bromwich has written persuasively on the relevance of placelessness to the nihilism at the psychic core of Hemingway's work, adding that placelessness is also 'a kind of deliverance for the writer'.[27] This state allows a free-floating exercise of personal, idiosyncratic, even transgressive needs put to the service of a life unanchored to the codes of permanent communities. What is remarkable in the case of Faulkner, however, is how similar needs were released by the opposite state—staying at home as a kind of deliverance.

If exile became for Joyce what Richard Ellmann calls a 'strategy of combat',[28] a fruitful way to measure the homeland by another, more alien world, Faulkner made staying at home his strategy of combat, and the measure he used was his own imagination, whose primary display of power is the extravagance of his art, that which made him different from his locale. Faulkner's most fruitful tension proved finally to be his resistance to the local.

Being a 'sensitive mind in the provinces' was an early explanation for Faulkner's ambiguous relationship to his place, and it is still relevant. In a place where even folk culture lacked any 'regularly assigned status or rôle for the writer', the exceptional young man, according to this model, is by his own lights an alien among friends and kin.[29] Without reading more trauma in that situation than is warranted, we can imagine that Faulkner's first serious attempts at writing would deliberately proclaim his 'difference'. *The Marble Faun* was Faulkner's 'lapsarian garden of modernity', writes Lewis P. Simpson, and in using the tools of modernism to counter the lostness, his art became a compulsion, a kind of sacred obligation to his novitiate.[30] There is nothing in the earliest work to indicate that Faulkner's notion of art bore any similarity to the genteel sort common enough in the South of his growing-up years. The producers of polite, sentimental and inspirational literature could not have found much in common with even the young Faulkner's intense, dense, smartly medievalized fables written for the woman he loved.

Even while his notion of the artist was extravagant and lofty, Faulkner at his best had the shrewd sense to keep his muse earthbound. The portentous and pretentious impulse meant that he was sanctioned to indulge his inordinate appetite for myth and symbol—for initiation rituals, creation stories, Orpheus myths, Christ stories, and the like—but a kind of country restraint would often lead him to neutralize the extravagance. If the snake is, declaratively, 'the old one, the ancient and accursed about the earth', his appearance is homely enough, trailing as he does 'the thin sick smell of rotting cucumbers'. Or when he decides to elevate the artist figure, he characteristically chooses permutations that, like Melville's, celebrate the unlikely, the unsung. Perhaps remembering Sophia Hawthorne's symbolic act at the Old Manse, Faulkner permits one Cecilia Farmer to scratch her name on the jailhouse window with her diamond, but the poignant artistic impulse is likened to 'the thin dried slime left by the passage of a snail'.[31]

And if he took his daemon seriously, according his art the right of priority over the sensibilities of friends, kin and any number of little old ladies, he could also, probably for strategic reasons, puncture the inflated image of himself as artist (calling himself a farmer, a horse-raiser). In *Mosquitoes*, his Huxleyan second novel, Faulkner distributed his aesthetic attitudes among several characters representing widely diverse theories of art; and even though it never coheres in its Jazz Age send-up of 'theme' novels, the minimal requirement for the artist comes when the author insinuates himself into that group as the 'little kind of black man': Faulkner names 'Faulkner' as 'liar by profession'. We might also remember 'Afternoon of a Cow', written in the aftermath of his greatest work, in which as 'Ernest V. Trueblood', Faulkner skewered his own proclivities for the pompous and magisterial mode by making himself the beshitted hero in a mock-romantic tale about the rescue of a cow from a pasture fire: 'Mr. Faulkner' ends up receiving 'the full discharge of the poor creature's afternoon of anguish and despair'. The cathartic climax is preserved, without the comic scatology, in *The Hamlet*, in which an idiot replaces the rôle of 'Mr. Faulkner'.[32]

Even before it escalated into a cultural phenomenon, the annual affair known as the Faulkner and Yoknapatawpha Conference was a hybrid of old-fashioned Chautauqua and M.L.A. symposium, held in Oxford, not because Ole Miss, its sponsor, is there, but because Faulkner was there. If its M.L.A. faction still vaguely insists—but with less compelling fervour each succeeding year—that Jefferson-Yoknapatawpha is not to be confused with Oxford-Lafayette, the Chautauqua types cheerfully perpetuate the confusion. By the time of the sixteenth annual conference in 1989, academic and commercial interests had found common cause to favour the Chautauquans. As the psycho-biography of Faulkner gradually reveals more and more of the dynamics that generated the art, it seems less and less relevant to separate the raw materials of his local geography and history from their imaginative uses in his fiction. Even before the advent of the Faulkner and Yoknapatawpha Conference, James B. Meriwether observed that 'what we know, what we can know, of Mississippi, will forever be modified by what he knew of it, and what he made of it in his fiction, in the created world of his art.'[33] Quite so.

In some palimpsestic way, Faulkner's town is both Oxford and Jefferson; as boutiques, motels, passable restaurants, and a savvy chamber of commerce have eased it onto the verge of the urban mainstream, its economic health has simultaneously preserved Oxford-as-Jefferson. It is a development that began forty years ago, when Hollywood technicians and support crews descended on the town soliciting home-grown co-operation in the filming of *Intruder in the Dust*. From bemused tolerance of Oxfordians toward those whose outside valuation of William Faulkner did not always and precisely match their own has evolved canny, no-nonsense promotion, a Ratliff-like willingness to *do business*. If, as Meriwether said, our very knowledge of Faulkner's place has been forever modified by his art, the place itself has validated that change.

Faulkner's true Penelope was not Flaubert, but it was art, an art that would deserve the lifeblood necessary to nourish it; and though Faulkner the man was occasionally conscious of having been born in 'a half savage country, out of date', Faulkner the writer, once he accepted that country as his *donnée*, never doubted that he could, like Pound's Mauberley, wring lilies from its acorn. When he writes in one of his poems, 'Though I be dead, / This earth that holds me fast will find me breath', the conventional Georgianism of the conception may disguise the resoluteness of the promise. Like Eudora Welty and other southern writers of his generation, Faulkner knew from experience that 'this earth' is suffocating as well as inspiriting and that its only permanent function lay in its transformation. With the substitution of 'art' for 'earth', Faulkner would supply a virtually unextinguishable flow of breath. Faulkner's Yoknapatawpha is sometimes less than lilies, but it is always more than acorns.

Faulkner's Fortunate Geography

NOTES

1. For biographical information see particularly Joseph Blotner, *Faulkner: A Biography*, 2 vols. (New York: Random House, 1974) and the revised and updated one-volume version (New York: Random House, 1984) and the relevant chapters in Michael Millgate, *The Achievement of William Faulkner* (New York: Random House, 1966). Of the interpretive lives I have been most helped by David Minter, *William Faulkner: His Life and Work* (Baltimore: Johns Hopkins University Press, 1980). The most valuable works on the contexts of Faulkner's life and career are two by Cleanth Brooks, *William Faulkner: The Yoknapatawpha Country* (New Haven: Yale University Press, 1963) and *William Faulkner: Toward Yoknapatawpha and Beyond* (New Haven: Yale University Press, 1978).
2. Jeremy Hooker, *Poetry of Place: Essays and Reviews 1970–1981* (Manchester: Carcanet Press, 1982), p. 66.
3. *Selected Letters of William Faulkner*, ed. Joseph Blotner (New York: Random House, 1977): September 1932; October 1932; August 1951; February 1935.
4. Edward Relph, *Place and Placelessness* (London: Pion, 1976): 'The places to which we are most committed may be the very centre of our lives, but they may also be oppressive and imprisoning. . . . There is not merely a fusion between person and place, but also a tension between them' (pp. 41–2).
5. *Selected Letters*: February 1935.
6. *Selected Letters*: February 1940; Winter 1946; November 1944; March 1947.
7. Robert Lowell, *Collected Prose*, ed., Robert Giroux (New York: Farrar, Straus & Giroux, 1987), p. 50.
8. Elmo Howell, 'William Faulkner and the Plain People of Yoknapatawpha County', *Journal of Mississippi History*, 24 (1962), 77.
9. Gary Lee Stonum, *Faulkner's Career: An Internal Literary History* (Ithaca: Cornell University Press, 1979), p. 30.
10. In two articles a geographer has convincingly demonstrated that Yoknapatawpha is neither a microcosm of the South—Elizabeth Kerr's position in *Yoknapatawpha: Faulkner's 'Little Postage Stamp of Native Soil'* (New York: Fordham University Press, 1969)—nor even, as Lowland South, this region in miniature, but one imaginatively envisioned 'as a specific location in the South'. See Charles S. Aiken, 'Faulkner's Yoknapatawpha County: Geographical Fact into Fiction', *Geographical Review*, 67 (January 1977), 1–21, and 'Faulkner's Yoknapatawpha County: A Place in the American South', *Geographical Review*, 69 (July 1979), 331–48. See a more theoretical article that also considers Faulkner's county, Phillip C. Muehrcke and Juliana O. Muehrcke, 'Maps in Literature', *Geographical Review*, 64 (July 1974), 317–38.
11. For a more detailed account of Faulknerian transposition in this

novel see John K. Simon, 'The Scene and the Imagery of Metamorphosis in *As I Lay Dying*', *Criticism*, 7 (1965), 1-22. See also an important segment in the relevant chapter in Robert Dale Parker, *Faulkner and the Novelistic Imagination* (Urbana: University of Illinois Press, 1985), pp. 31-46, and James H. Justus, 'Hemingway and Faulkner: Vision and Repudiation', *Kenyon Review*, n.s. 7 (Fall 1985), 1-14.
12. Quoted in Hooker, *Poetry of Place*, p. 159.
13. Gaston Bachelard, *The Poetics of Space* (New York: Orion Press, 1964), p. 120.
14. *Faulkner in the University*, ed. Frederick L. Gwynn and Joseph Blotner (Charlottesville: University of Virginia Press, 1959), p. 59.
15. Yi-Fu Tuan, *Space and Place: The Perspective of Experience* (Minneapolis: University of Minnesota Press, 1977), p. 136.
16. Daniel Aaron, 'The South in American History', in *The South and Faulkner's Yoknapatawpha: The Actual and the Apocryphal*, ed. Evans Harrington and Ann J. Abadie (Jackson: University Press of Mississippi, 1977), p. 19; Robert Penn Warren, 'Not Local Color', *Virginia Quarterly Review*, 8 (January 1932), 160. See also Max Putzel, *Genius of Place: William Faulkner's Triumphant Beginnings* (Baton Rouge: L.S.U. Press, 1985), p. 137.
17. William Faulkner, *The Marble Faun* (Boston: Four Seas, 1924), pp. 6-7; William Faulkner, *Mayday*, ed. Carvel Collins (Notre Dame: University of Notre Dame Press, 1978), pp. 47-8.
18. William Faulkner, *Collected Stories* (New York: Random House, 1950), p. 899.
19. William Faulkner, *Flags in the Dust* (New York: Random House, 1973), pp. 267-68.
20. *Mayday*, pp. 78-9.
21. William Faulkner, *The Town* (New York: Random House, 1957), pp. 315-16.
22. William Faulkner, *Intruder in the Dust* (New York: Random House, 1948), pp. 151-53.
23. William Faulkner, 'Mississippi', in *Essays, Speeches, and Public Letters*, ed. James B. Meriwether (New York: Random House, 1965), p. 43.
24. William Faulkner, *Absalom, Absalom!* (New York: Random House, 1936), pp. 303, 258.
25. James B. Meriwether, 'Faulkner's Mississippi', *Mississippi Quarterly*, 25 (Spring 1972 Supplement), 19.
26. The reliable text of 'Kentucky: May: Saturday' is included in *Essays, Speeches, and Public Letters*, pp. 52-61.
27. David Bromwich, 'Hemingway's Valor', *Grand Street*, 7 (Winter 1988), 211.
28. Richard Ellmann, *James Joyce*, rev. ed. (New York: Oxford, 1982), p. 110.
29. John Mclachan, 'No Faulkner in Metropolis', in *Southern Renascence: The Literature of the Modern South*, ed. Louis D. Rubin, Jr., and

Robert D. Jacobs (Baltimore: Johns Hopkins University Press, 1966), pp. 109–11.
30. Lewis P. Simpson, 'Faulkner and the Legend of the Artist', in *Faulkner: Fifty Years After 'The Marble Faun'*, ed. George H. Wolfe (University: University of Alabama Press, 1976), pp. 79–89.
31. William Faulkner, *Go Down, Moses* (New York: Random House, 1942), p. 329; 'The Jail' prologue to Act Three of *Requiem for a Nun* (New York: Random House, 1951), pp. 252–53.
32. William Faulkner, 'Afternoon of a Cow', in *Uncollected Stories*, ed. Joseph Blotner (New York: Random House, 1979), p. 430.
33. Meriwether, 'Faulkner's "Mississippi" ', 23.

2
Modernist Faulkner?
A Yoknapatawpha Trilogy

by A. ROBERT LEE

> You write a story to tell about people, man in his constant struggle with his own heart, with the hearts of others, or with his environment. It's man in the ageless, eternal struggles which we inherit and we go through as though they'd never happened before, shown for a moment in a dramatic instant of the furious moment of being alive, that's all any story is. You catch this fluidity which is human life and you focus a light on it and you stop it long enough for people to be able to see it. . . .
> —*Faulkner in The University: Class Conferences at The University of Virginia 1957–1958*[1]

1

When, in November 1950, news of his Nobel Prize was first 'phoned through to Oxford, Mississippi, from Stockholm, Faulkner appears to have reacted with an equanimity rare even by his own standards.[2] The prospect of the cash pleased him well enough (he spoke of getting work done on the family home, though in fact much of the payment eventually went into endowing black college scholarships). Whether, however, it was genuine unperturbedness or more a well-taken foreboding about becoming a personality, it took him no time at all to plead that 'farming' duties would prevent him crossing the Atlantic to receive the award in person. The plaudits which in quick order gathered about his head, by contrast, knew no such restraint. At one end, and doubtless

Modernist Faulkner? A Yoknapatawpha Trilogy

born out of local familiarity with the reticent side of his nature, there appeared the banner headline of the *Eagle*, his hometown newspaper—'BILL FAULKNER'S GOTTA LET OXFORD BE PROUD OF A NOBEL PRIZE WINNER'.[3] At another, and in another country, there was his acclaim by Gustaf Hellström, President of the Swedish Academy and himself a writer of distinction, as the 'unrivalled master of all living British and American novelists'.[4] Oxford, Stockholm or elsewhere, Faulkner had established an ascendancy neither he nor his publishers and family could ever previously have assumed.

Doubts, to be sure, persisted, then as now. Could this act of canonization erase all the different cavils, reservations, and even outright hostility, to which his fiction had been subject virtually since he began his career as a novelist with *Soldier's Pay* (1926)?[5] Further, it took no great feat of memory to recall that without Malcolm Cowley's creation of *The Portable Faulkner* in 1946, his reputation may well have remained at the kind of low ebb of the 1930s when few of his books could be found in print and those read more for curiosity value than anything else. Cowley it was who demonstrated that Yoknapatawpha amounted to 'one connected story', a 'living pattern', nothing less than 'a permanent state of consciousness'.[6] More generally, his Introduction and selection of extracts also won Faulkner a fundamental and much needed renewal of credibility, a writer whose Southernness hitherto had meant little more than a kind of regional American sub-world in which the author's supposed penchant for the gratuitously violent and sexual, and for characters who verged on the pathological, could find free expression. In this, too, Southern had served to link him to Poe, Faulkner as the perpetuator of a too blatant Gothic or melodramatic repertoire. It also became unflattering shorthand for his style, one almost routinely thought disfigured by its run-on sentences, excited imagery and often contrived word-formations and italicizations. Faulkner's rise can hardly be said to have come about without odds.

The award of the Nobel Prize may not entirely have removed these misgivings, but it did stop them assuming automatic pride of place. No longer could Faulkner be dealt with simply as some baroque or fevered regionalist from below the Mason-Dixon line. Here, rather, was an American writer of genuine consequence, Yoknapatawpha's only begetter as nothing less than a decisive modern literary presence. Yoknapatawpha itself was to be invoked, without apology, as an imagined world fully the equal of Hawthorne's New England or Dickens's London or Hardy's Wessex. Faulkner's violence, furthermore, it came to be seen, had about it a rationale, a necessity even, in the overall epic and dynastic formulation of Yoknapatawpha. This was anything but shock for its own sake or arch thrill-mongering. Faulkner's styles of narrative, in turn, would also win a better appreciation, be it his uses of memory or his weave of the formal and the vernacular or even the often elusive temper of much of his humour. It could at last be said and without distortion that Faulkner, in company with Hemingway and Fitzgerald, had no more than assumed his due place in bestriding early twentieth-century American fiction.

Generally agreed as was his right to a top billing, however, opinion continues to differ markedly on the imaginative workings of Faulkner's fiction, its modes of seizing and holding the attention. In this respect one issue most especially has been of note, and not merely on account of some prim obsession with categorization or genre. It arises out of the odd, almost defiantly contradictory, interaction in his story-telling between what broadly (and allowing for all competing definition) might be termed the traditional and the modern or modernist. For Faulkner, under a variety of guises, has widely been perceived to be both, on the one hand an ancestral, near bardic, teller of tales, and on the other, in his ways of telling, a voice uncannily and almost prophetically contemporary. How best to understand, or more to the immediate point, how best to take the measure of, this paradox, this seeming disjuncture?

'Man in his constant struggle with his own heart', 'Man in the ageless, eternal struggles'. The phrases, unmistakeably, bear Faulkner's insignia, humanness as ritualized cycle and repetition. Not that Faulkner, here or elsewhere, ever stepped free of his own wholly specific sense of history: Mississippi, slavery and the wilful domination of white over

Modernist Faulkner? A Yoknapatawpha Trilogy

black, the legacy of Sherman and Civil War defeat, Bible Christianity, a determining cycle of crop and weather, and a population extending from Chickasaw Indians to blacks to a hierarchy of settler whites and their descendants—this latter a mix of would-be gentry, traders and townspeople, and different 'poor white' smallholders and their clans. Beyond, too, the Yoknapatawpha Faulkner made over from his literal Lafayette County in north Mississippi, there can also be heard the footfalls of other inherited dispensations. These include the Old Testament, the Greek Tragedies, Shakespeare, Conrad and the great Russians, and from his American forbears, no lesser nay-sayers than Hawthorne and Melville. Nor, of writers from his own time, did Faulkner's enthusiasm for Camus happen by chance.[7] They share a kind of stoic defiance in the face of an absurdist common human destiny, an affinity which no doubt helps explain the alacrity with which Faulkner was also taken up in post-occupation France by Sartre and Simone de Beauvoir in *Les Temps Modernes*.[8] By these and associated lights Faulkner truly appears the very custodian of tradition, or in his own phrasing, of the 'ageless' and 'eternal' and 'constant'.

But for all of this, Faulkner has matchingly been associated with a quite countervailing current. Did he not, as the early poetry of *The Marble Faun* (1924) and many of his first stories for good or ill bear witness, serve an apprenticeship to Swinburne and in turn to the *symboliste* constellation of Verlaine, Baudelaire, Rimbaud and Mallarmé? Is not the hand of Beardsley and *The Yellow Book* to be discerned in his own youthful line-drawings and designs? Was not Sherwood Anderson, too, an important founding mentor, to his own generation if not subsequently a beacon of the new (as Faulkner's *Times-Picayune* pieces of 1925 which later became his *New Orleans Sketches* bear affectionate witness)? Of still greater consequence, did not Faulkner take infinitely more than simply passing cognizance of incontrovertible moderns like Joyce and Eliot, not to mention Freud and his different *dicta* and findings?

In truth the will to art existed inside Faulkner well ahead of Oxford or Mississippi or the South, an art, too, resolutely pledged to the modern, to making new (and in new ways) the Southern legacy he knew awaited his powers of transformation. His experiments with memory and association, with viewpoint and the break-up of linear time-sequence and chronology, as with other reflexive aspects of his fiction, quite unmistakeably bespeak a modernist inclination. The remarks in his University of Virginia interview, thereby, of the writer's being able to show 'for a moment' the 'furious motion of being alive' and of 'focusing a light', modest as may appear but hard not to think other than nicely disingenuous, also point the way. 'That's all a story is', for sure, amounts to understatement with a purpose. For however much he liked to affect the farmer, the Mississippi horse-trader or the like setting down as if incidentally yarns garnered from backcountry Mississippi, Faulkner from the outset knew himself to be a conscious participant in the emerging imaginative directions of his own century—nothing less, in fact, than one of its essential innovators.

Faulkner's Yoknapatawpha fiction, then, whether best construed as a species of ancient writ, or as self-avowed modernism, or even more intriguingly as an elusive combination of both as I want myself to suggest, in this respect (as, given the plethora of criticism and scholarship, not a little dauntingly in others) continues to invite debate. Nowhere, too, has it done so more than in the case of three of his best established novels, *The Sound and the Fury* (1929), *As I Lay Dying* (1930) and *Absalom, Absalom!* (1936).[9] Each of these, as Faulkner many times insisted, palpably enacts a drama, a body of made-over events, yet each, as he equally insisted, in no uncertain terms calls attention to the act of narrative as matchingly and in itself an imaginative drama. Be it, thus, the saga of the Compsons, or of the Bundrens, or of Sutpen's Hundred, Faulkner at one and the same time invites our witness both to a unique increment of Yoknapatawpha and to his own modes of inscribing and patterning that story. Yoknapatawpha, accordingly, whatever else it signifies, also serves as a means by which the old or inherited becomes enclosed in the new, the ancient in the modern. That process, and its implications for a modernist Faulkner, lies at the centre of the present consideration.[10]

Modernist Faulkner? A Yoknapatawpha Trilogy

2

Given these general bearings, Faulkner's own well-known account of *The Sound and the Fury* offers an especially pertinent point of departure:

> It began with the picture of the little girl's muddy drawers, climbing that tree to look in the parlor window with her brothers that didn't have the courage to climb the tree waiting to see what she saw. And I tried first to tell it with one brother, and that wasn't enough. That was Section One. I tried with another brother, and that wasn't enough. That was Section Two. I tried the third brother, because Caddy was still to me too beautiful and too moving to reduce her to telling what was going on, that it would be more passionate to see her through someone's else's eyes, I thought. And that failed and I tried myself—the fourth section—to tell what happened, and I still failed.[11]

Four versions there may be, but the history which centres on, and about, Caddie Compson, and to which Benjy, Quentin, Jason and Dilsey offer their complementary testimony, in one sense could not offer a clearer or more tangible set of happenings. From the origins begun in Quentin MacLachan's flight from Culloden, through to the deal struck with Ikkemotubbe about the Chickasaw land which will eventually become the Compson property in the middle of Jefferson, and on into the events for which Caddie's 'muddy drawers' serve as the icon, the story unfolds as a quite inexorable drama. For does not *The Sound and the Fury* enact that most familiar Southern paradigm, the fall of a warring family or house, a ritualistic cycle of destruction fully at one with the Macbethian implications of the title? Here, across all four sections, is truly dynastic fare, the great generational ceremonies of innocence, sexual initiation, marriage and death worked into an unfolding whole. Further, such a story written under Southern auspices has a special resonance. Family, with all its inlaid tensions of lineage, honour, intimacy and division, has long been one of the fundamental story-resources in Southern literary tradition, from, say, Poe's 'The Fall of the House of Usher' (1839) and Twain's *Huckleberry Finn* (1884), on to and beyond, say, Tennessee Williams's *The Glass Menagerie* (1944) and Eudora Welty's *Delta Wedding* (1946). Faulkner's novel both draws on and at the same time particularizes that tradition, a story recognizably of a genre yet utterly its own creation.

But to stress too insistently this dynamic of story, powerful without question though it is, would be akin to remembering *Moby-Dick* only for the whale-hunt or *Ulysses* only for the outward show of a Dublin day. The greater effect of *The Sound and the Fury* lies precisely in subjecting the Compson collapse to Faulkner's 'trying to tell it' four times over and then in the mediating interplay of those tellings. 'Failure' may have been Faulkner's own professed estimate of the result, but to a considerable extent that can be thought an author's familiar lament at the shortfall between the would-be ideal achievement and its inevitably lesser execution. His readers, certainly, for the most part have taken the more charitable view. If sometimes hard put, at first, to establish bearings (especially in Benjy's section), far more rather than less have been won over by the unbroken virtuosity of Faulkner's telling. In this respect, quite inextricably, the issue of the novel's modernism or otherwise again comes into play.

Firstly, Section One, Benjy's section, seemingly offers the very instance of modernist narration, an opening instalment unapologetically 'difficult' and which develops its perspective on the Compsons in a manner not unrelated to that deployed in 'The Waste Land' or *Ulysses*. Like these landmarks, too, Faulkner's 'difficulty' cannot be thought other than intrinsic to his story's overall meaning. That is, as the tale of the Compsons is released through the back-and-forth sense data of the mentally retarded Benjy, so Faulkner seeks our recognition of an old story having been put under drastically new rules. Instead of the formal continuity of cause and effect, Faulkner makes his operating levers those of discontinuity, time-shift, a dialogue or collectivity of voices speaking across linear chronology. Interstices are left to be filled in by the aiding and abetting reader, a format which works in the manner of a collagist or cubist design.

Benjy's fifteen flashbacks might so be said to make up points in a continuum, a collage of moments whose linear connectedness remains tacit and of a subsidiary importance. In excising conventional linkage in this way, Benjy's account in *The Sound and the Fury* genuinely achieves fresh ground by,

Modernist Faulkner? A Yoknapatawpha Trilogy

among other things, the establishment of a different mode of novelistic time, the use of basic sensations of sight or smell as indices of human memory, and, allowing for the likes of Dostoevsky's *The Idiot* and the figure of Stevie in Conrad's *The Secret Agent*, the creation of a new kind of self in fiction. Benjy's life, like any other, in one sense can be granted an ascertainable beginning, middle and end. But, given his mental state, he himself does not, or patently cannot, experience it that way. Nor, as Faulkner boldly recognized at the outset, can we, and duly adapted his telling to match, an old problem as might be thought exhilaratingly given a modernist solution.

This issue of time, and therefore sequence, is crucial. Calendar dates are not exactly denied us—the overall Easter Weekend frame of 6, 7 and 8 April 1928, the death of Damuddy in 1898, the change of Benjy's name from its original Maury in 1900, the sale of Benjy's pasture for a golf course in order to pay for Quentin to be sent to Harvard in 1909, Caddie's seduction by Dalton Ames and then her marriage to Sydney Head in 1910, Quentin's suicide and funeral also in 1910, the death of Mr. Compson in 1912, and Benjy's castration in 1913. But all of this change Faulkner discloses fugitively, as if, in the circumstances, conventionally marked time can no longer do proper service. Time-switches, accordingly, are to be indicated by italicization, by the same character speaking variously as child and adult, by the evolving roster of Benjy's black minders (in order Versh, T.P., Dilsey and her husband Roskus, and Frony and her son Luster), and by Benjy's alternately favouring or disfavouring association of Caddie with flowers, water, jimson weed and fire. Each of these key motifs, like Faulkner's use of the family mirror as a reflector of past and present or the golfball-caddy-fence cluster, resonates one in terms of the other but never without the implication of an actual and ongoing time-scheme. Above all, in the ensuing sections as in his own, Benjy's wail lays down the strongest marker of change, as for instance at Caddie's use of perfume (the implications of which Faulkner leaves to us), or at the mention of her name long after she has fled. His eventual final wail in Dilsey's section when Luster drives him the wrong way round the monument of the eyeless Confederate soldier in Jefferson thus completes the pattern, an end to all literal Compson time, an end to the march of dynasty.

The other major innovatory dimension of Benjy's section lies in Faulkner's voicing, narrative as a form of uniquely ongoing colloquium, things said, echoed and remembered, as equal in importance with things actually done.[12] Voices, in Bakhtin's phrase, for Faulkner here truly do work 'dialogically', each in shaping tension with another, whether the hypochondriac Bascomb whine of Mrs. Compson or the ingratiation of Uncle Maury, or Dilsey's black mothering assuagement and reprimand, or the respective idioms of the three 'normal' Compson siblings, or, crucially, Benjy's own mnemonic utterances ('*Caddie smelled like trees*', for instance, or '*I hate rain*', or '*His name's Benjy now, Caddy said*'). We also have to agree to Faulkner's fiction that Benjy can in fact 'speak' at all, an 'I' inscribed upon the page only as an accord between writer and reader. He assumes voice, and we give sanction to it, in obvious defiance of his inability to use conventional human logic or syntax. Not the least part of the modernist in Faulkner is his awareness, under these conditions, of an altered rôle for the reader.

Yet for all its fine complication, Benjy's section as often noted also offers the purest of records, a register of what on his part has to amount to undeliberated immediacies (underlined, notably, in the concluding sentence about how 'the dark' goes in 'smooth, bright shapes, like it always does, even when Caddie says that I have been asleep'). Our part in the story, however, has to be anything but undeliberated, an invitation to decipherment and reconstruction which yields simplicity only through complexity and an old story only through our willingness to enter into a new kind of storytelling.

One dwells upon Benjy's section because, so determinedly, it resorts to these modernist arrangements. Only slightly less so, does Quentin's section. If Benjy is all sensory impression, undeliberatedness, Quentin is quite the opposite, the Harvard senior trapped to the point of collapse by an impossible Southern rhetoric of timeless chivalry and timeless purity as he would have them embodied in himself and Caddie. That contrast gathers further point in Faulkner's

Modernist Faulkner? A Yoknapatawpha Trilogy

having made Benjy's time-present his birthday, and 2 June 1910, the day of Quentin's narration, his death-day. The portrait of Quentin is the portrait of a mind losing all belief in clock or calendar time or in any of the conventional and for most minds necessary divisions between pastness and presentness. Hence his Confederate grandfather's watch, smeared in his own blood as he tries to destroy time and an implied reference-back to Caddie's loss of virginity, merges into the jeweller's watches (none of which for Quentin tells the 'right' time), and they in turn into his own body as a sun-dial ('I stepped into sunlight, finding my shadow again'), and that into the factory whistles, and they into the clock of the Unitarian steeple, and that, finally, into the timelessness he craves by drowning. Just as Benjy embodies, as it were, merest consciousness and no more, so, as Faulkner tells it, Quentin suffers a consciousness too intensely active for him to bear. Again, too, Faulkner creates a mode of telling to suit.

Similarly, Faulkner has Dalton Ames collapse into Gerald Bland for Quentin, as anachronistically he fights for his sister's honour. Deacon, the black dormitory porter, equally becomes one with black figures from Quentin's Jefferson past. Above all, the little Italian girl (whom Quentin explicitly addresses as 'sister' and is accused of kidnapping) metamorphizes into the young Caddie. Nor can Quentin separate his own affair with Natalie from Caddy and her pregnancy, a swirl of images calling up menstruation, muddiedness and purification, and his one-time death-pact with his sister. Likewise to the point, Shreve, his Canadian room-mate, is made to ask whether he is dressed for a funeral or a marriage, an allusion to the clothes Quentin will go on to clean in preparation for his own death and an implied contrast with Caddie's 'muddy drawers' which rankle so destructively in his mind as the sign of her defloration and pregnancy. In his unsequenced sense of things, he thinks back to telling his father he has committed incest with his sister, as if, impossibly, he can put an end to all change and growth not of his own making. Faulkner's 'i temporary' becomes for him intolerable, resolvable only by a last transition into permanent stillness below water which he anticipates in his discussion with the boys who are fishing and in such words as 'I could feel water beyond the twilight, smell'. All time thus comes to coexist for him equally, as Faulkner underscores by having much of the latter parts of his section stand as one-off lines separated from larger sentences or paragraphs. Once more a modernist design has yielded an old story, that of the break-up of a mind.

From there, *The Sound and the Fury* moves back towards more traditional narration, as if, among other things, to complete the possible ways by which we might grasp the Compson story. That, in itself, could well be thought a species of modernist joke, a tacit or built-in parody of our wish for the 'straight' story-line. Jason's section, at any rate, that of the only sane Compson as his Bascomb mother insists, brings us back to earth with a jolt. His brute clichés ('Once a bitch always a bitch' or 'jews are alright as individuals but . . .'), like his grimly comic detestation of Southern 'honour' (' "I haven't got much pride, I can't aford it with a kitchen full of niggers to feed and robbing the state asylum of its star freshman" '), gives us realism with a vengeance. His own fate in becoming a false Jason, the adventurer cheated by Quentin, Caddie's daughter, after having spent a lifetime cheating her, tells a bastard and at times wickedly parodic version of the myth of the Golden Fleece. His indeed is the worldly life (' "Blood, I says, governors and generals. It's a damn good thing we never had any kings and presidents; we'd all be down there at Jackson chasing butterflies" '), and Faulkner once again adjusts the telling of his story to suit. But no more than the sections given to Benjy or Quentin does Jason's give the whole account, despite all its mean, uncompromising, factuality, still the story only in part.

Dilsey's section, equally, Faulkner casts in more conventional narrative form, the section he acknowledges to have 'tried myself' and the only one of the four told in the third-person. Thematically, Dilsey gives human embodiment to the Easter sermon preached in her own black church, a signifier of life over death and the open Bible as against the closed Bible of Mrs. Compson (' "Hush. Dilsey's got you" ', she tells a wailing Benjy towards the end). She it is, further, who especially carries forth the Easter message of family, not only in the care of her own kin but in the care of the

Modernist Faulkner? A Yoknapatawpha Trilogy

most vulnerable Compsons—Benjy, foremost, then Caddie and Quentin as children, and in her turn, Caddie's daughter Quentin. To Dilsey, too, falls the burden of continuity ('They will prevail' and ' "I seed de first and de last" '), human endurance as against the destructive wheel of the Compsons's sound and fury. Controversy has much arisen over Dilsey. Is she simply an Aunt Jemima, some stereotyped black mammy?[13] That debate, passionately engaged in by a critical readership raised on Civil Rights and beyond, for present purposes belongs elsewhere. Faulkner himself, it cannot be doubted, clearly conceived her as exemplary, a saving figure of compassion in the face of fatal human division. Even so, 'her' account, too, its idiom black, oral, and shot through with echoes of churchgoing and spirituals, can still only incompletely tell 'what happened'. That is so, furthermore, however much she sees the Compsons in terms of Christian parable with betrayers and fallen angels and none more so than the Benjy who carries his broken narcissus in hand and howls one last martyred time as Luster drives him the wrong way round the Jefferson town square.

Perhaps the Appendix, which in current editions appears at the beginning, holds a best clue. Its roll-call of all the players in the Compson drama, from Ikkemotubbe ('A dispossessed American king') and Andrew Jackson ('A Great White Father with a sword') through to the first and last of the Compsons and their black co-family, provides a species of historical bedrock, the working human data for all that occurs. But in transposing the story four ways, and into fiction which rests neither entirely on the new nor entirely on the old but on a quite prodigious overlap of both, *The Sound and the Fury* offers its own acknowledgement of the impossibility of any one final, authorized version. That, too, may also amount to the truest measure of Faulkner himself, the modernist within the Yoknapatawpha story-teller of old and the story-teller of old within the Yoknapatawpha modernist, nothing if not a most singular coexistence.

3

In the case of *As I Lay Dying*, Faulkner as interviewee again yields an opening perspective. When asked about technique in the novel by Jean Stein for the *Paris Review*, his reply ran as follows:

> I simply imagined a group of people and subjected them to the simple universal natural catastrophes, which are flood and fire, with a simple natural motive to give direction to their progress.[14]

A similar question at the University of Virginia elicited the following response:

> I took this family, and subjected them to the two greatest catastrophes which man can suffer—flood and fire, that's all. That was simple *tour de force*. That was written in six weeks without changing a word because I knew from the first where that was going.[15]

On both occasions, and whether he meant to cover his steps or not, he typically offered something less than the whole truth of the matter. The novel indeed can be said to rework a story old or ancestral in genre, with intertextual allusions back to the Books of Genesis and Isaiah and to any number of classic journey epics. A Pilgrim's Progress, a rite of burial, a Voyage Thither in Herman Melville's phrase,[16] none is to be denied. But as the story unfolds through its more than fifty monologues, each chorically linked into the other and into a Yoknapatawpha background in which the grotesque and comic shade almost imperceptibly into the poignant and even tragic, 'simply imagined' would be almost the last description to come to mind. For, yet once again, Faulkner's art displays a wholly modernist virtuosity, 'universal natural catastrophes', if one will, 'flood and fire' and 'a simple natural motive', in addition, but shaped throughout by the most striking innovations of design.

For good reason, much of the commentary on *As I Lay Dying* has begun with Addie, the expiring life force who controls the Bundren orbit of Anse, Cash, Darl, Jewel, Dewey Dell and Vardaman. Each creates a definition of her—for Anse the accuser of his own wheedling meanness of spirit

Modernist Faulkner? A Yoknapatawpha Trilogy

('I am a luckless man. I have ever been.', 'We would be beholden to no man.'), for Cash the mother to whom duty is owed, for Darl the dying prop to his sanity, for Jewel the ever-favouring and so weak parent, for Dewey Dell the absent helpmate in her unwanted pregnancy, for Vardaman in his child's eye Nature's life-figure ('My mother is a fish'), for Cora Tull the best baker of cakes 'in this section', and for Dr. Peabody the patient Anse has called him to too late (' "Well, Miss Addie. . . . How are you sister?" '). None, however, defines her as she does herself, comfortless, alone and, above all, riven by the gap between words and things ('I would think how words go straight up in a thin line, quick and harmless, and how terribly doing goes along the earth'). To regard language this way, as arbitrary hieroglyph, smacks of a Barthesian or Derridean prospectus, words as contingent ultimately on little or no more than themselves. Addie 'speaks' in despite of speech's meaninglessness for her, a condition only the modernist in Faulkner would ever have chosen so emphatically to recognize. Not that Addie, herself, of course, remains other than the figure of the novel, the schoolteacher who fearing spinsterdom marries Anse Bundren, mothers four children by him, and one, Jewel, by the Rev. Whitfield, and who watches Cash build her own coffin in preparation for the blackly comic journey to the burying ground.

Each of the other soliloquies takes on meaning in relation to Addie, an irony in that herself dying or dead and encoffined she can give rise to so much life from those around her. The ironic, however, hardly surprises in a context where a woman at once so married yet so exiled from love should go to her burial clad in wedding dress and veil (the latter to cover the holes driven by Vardaman through the coffin and into her face), the eternal bride but also the exhausted body of wife and mother. Nor does it surprise that in the supposed high ceremony of death, her corpse should unceremoniously be ferried to Jefferson in a borrowed cart, be upturned in a flood, be accidently almost cremated, and be hovered over by waiting buzzards, and all at the hands of her dutiful but patently ramshackle and ill-assorted family. The soliloquies which witness to her, furthermore, a syndrome of voices only partly comprehending of the whole, are themselves given a parodic finale in the words ' "Meet Mrs. Bundren" ' as Anse presents his new 'duck-shaped' wife. They also remind us that 'story', in anything like completeness, for Faulkner always resides in the competition of the witnessing involved, that the full meaning of the journey from the Bundren homestead to Tull's ford to Mottson to Gillespie's barn to Jefferson will for ever elude the single definition. History, 'what happened', in *As I Lay Dying* or elsewhere in Faulkner, thus again declares itself to lie neither in the gift of one set of voices nor of another, but in the mutuality of all those on offer. In this respect, also again, Faulkner the story-teller from an older tradition shares company with Faulkner the modernist.

Each of the Bundren soliloquies, nonetheless, do their part. Cash, who makes the coffin 'on the bevel' and who personifies the search for 'balance' even though it literally costs him a leg, bespeaks a first-born's sense of family obligation. Darl, whose psychic register is the keenest, who knows whose son Jewel is (in all its Hawthorneian implication), who typically spots his father's inability to sweat and his pathetic attempt to arrange the cover on Addie's bed, who recognizes Dewey Dell's condition almost as soon as she does herself, also seeks to make articulate the devastating inward cost of a mother's death to the extent of setting fire to her hearse in Gillespie's barn and of dealing with events only through an insanity that forces him to see himself as a self outside himself ('Darl is our brother, our brother Darl'. . . . "Yes yes yes yes yes yes yes yes." '). Jewel knows only the vocabulary of will, objectified in his loved and sublime horse which Anse trades for a new cart. Dewey Dell, slow with words herself ('I feel like a wet seed in the hot blind earth') becomes their repeated sexual victim, whether as a result of those spoken by Lafe at cotton-picking time or by the pharmacist MacGowan. For Vardaman, words, soliloquizing, stand at one remove from experience, as in his child's identification of the fish with his mother's need to take in air or in his interpretation of the buzzards more as playthings than emissaries of death. 'They come from some place out in Yoknapatawpha county, trying to get to Jefferson with it', observes one of the bemused

Modernist Faulkner? A Yoknapatawpha Trilogy

townsfolk as the caravan reaches its journey's end. He speaks nothing less than the truth, summarizes nothing less than the plot. But for everything else that remains to be said, everything else that makes for a modern imagining of an ancient story of 'family' and 'flood and fire', we must turn to Faulkner's other speakers, Bundren and non-Bundren alike. For only as a novel of voices each made new out of old can the right measure be established of *As I Lay Dying*.

4

In turning to *Absalom, Absalom!*, once more a much cited observation by Faulkner himself offers an irresistible starting-point. The occasion was another of his University of Virginia class sessions:

> Q. Mr. Faulkner, in *Absalom, Absalom!* does any one of the people who talk about Sutpen have the right view, or is it more or less a case of thirteen ways of looking at a blackbird with none of them right?
> A. That's it exactly. I think that no one individual can look at truth. It blinds you. You look at it and you see one phase of it. Someone else looks at it and sees a slightly awry phase of it. But taken all together, the truth is in what they saw though nobody saw the truth intact. So these are true as far as Miss Rosa and as Quentin saw it. Quentin's father saw what he believed was truth, that was all he saw. But the old man was himself a little too big for people no greater in stature than Quentin and Miss Rosa and Mr. Compson to see all at once. It would perhaps have taken perhaps a wiser or more tolerant or more sensitive or more thoughtful person to see him as he was. It was, as you say, thirteen ways of looking at a blackbird. But the truth, I would like to think, comes out, that when the reader has read all these thirteen different ways of looking at the blackbird, the reader has his own fourteenth image of that blackbird which I would like to think is the truth.[17]

Faulkner must have thought himself unexpectedly blessed in so good a question, not to mention in Wallace Stevens's blackbird. What better terms in which to explain his conception of Sutpen 'as he was', the upstart West Virginian possessed of his Grand Design of dynasty and a figure as much out of myth as history? At the same time, too, if somewhat less expressly, it gave Faulkner the chance to indicate something of the modernism of his own 'telling' in *Absalom, Absalom!*, a tale literally old as (or at least out of) the hills but made over into the new.

None of Faulkner's Yoknapatawpha novels can be said to make the process of story-telling itself so insistent a motif as *Absalom, Absalom!*, be it indeed standard-bearers like *The Sound and the Fury* and *As I Lay Dying*, or *Sartoris* (1929) which first enfables Yoknapatawpha, or *Light in August* (1932) with its parallel transcriptions of the lives of Joe Christmas and Lena Grove, or the mock-epic Snopes trilogy of *The Hamlet* (1940), *The Town* (1957) and *The Mansion* (1959), or the parabular *Go Down Moses* (1942). The Sutpen history unravels by increment and recapitulation, by interrogation and hearsay, at every turn propelled forward by a rare enactive energy. The four principal tellers and questioners—Rosa Coldfield, Mr. Compson, Quentin Compson and Shreve McCannon—so become both participant narrators and figures of our own impatience to have the story conclude, or at least come to rest. The novel in one sense indeed does come to rest: dead himself at the hands of Wash Jones, Sutpen's dream of lineage, too, is finally mocked in the idiot figure of Jim Bond. But *Absalom, Absalom!* also seeks to deny conclusion, Faulkner's thirteen or more ways of 'seeing' Sutpen for ever left in play as Quentin and Shreve summon up the story's ghosts from their chill Harvard dormitory. The novel thus works as a double-helix, in one incarnation linear, accelerated, an unfolding according to cause and effect, and in the other cross-plied, speculative, actively modernist in its resistance precisely to any final account.

This binary quality shows through in each component of the telling of the story. Costumed in her 'eternal black' and 'talking in that grim haggard amazed voice' to Quentin in December 1909, Rosa Coldfield opens the account by alluding to a past literally sealed inside the decaying Sutpen mansion. Faulkner casts her account in telegraphese, as if to imply how much will be required by way of gloss in the surrounding and subsequent text. *'This demon'*, she calls Sutpen, to which Quentin, her compelled auditor, adds

Modernist Faulkner? A Yoknapatawpha Trilogy

out of quiet thunderclap he would abrupt (man-horse-demon) upon a scene peaceful and decorous as a schoolprize water color, faint sulphur-reek still in hair clothes and beard. . . .

Sutpen as devil, a malign Jehovah willing Sutpen's Hundred into being to his own version of 'Let there be Light', offers a key coloration for all the 'plot' that then ensues. In Rosa's imagining, only as some Dixie hillboy Satan can Sutpen and his effect on the course of her life be glossed: his arrival 'out of nowhere' in Yoknapatawpha in 1833, the accompaniment of his French-speaking black slaves from Haiti, his marriage to her sister Ellen in 1838, the birth of Henry in 1839 and Ellen in 1841, the willed and boarded-up death of her father in his attic on account of the Civil War, and her implacable sense of insult at being asked to experiment in begetting a son. Faulkner, in effect, tells two stories, one in terms of the other, that to be elicited as 'fact' in all its supposed logic and sequence, and that which resonates in the mesmerized feelings and mind of a 64-year-old Jefferson spinster talking half-crazily to the 25-year-old Quentin at the turn of the present century.

As an overlay to Rosa's impressionistic fury we have Mr. Compson's account, variously relayed as reminiscences offered on the family porch, as letters, as information recalled by Quentin in Harvard. Mr. Compson helps establish an unmythic Sutpen, with a rationale to his actions—the rejection at the doorway, the certification of respectability by the marriage with Ellen ('[Sutpen] wanted . . . the two names, the stainless wife and the unimpeachable father-in-law, on the licence, the patent'), the Confederate war service, and the moves he made to resolve the fatal triangulation of Judith, Henry and Charles Bon. The ingredients for disaster are laid bare, whether Sutpen's own will to a male line or the especially Southern phobia of incest and miscegenation. Mr. Compson supplies the details of the Haitian and New Orleans connection, the analogies between the Compson and the Sutpen dynasties, and the rôle of Bon's mother and her lawyer, all again 'fact'.

He also, however, in a trope which calls up Hawthorne's 'The Custom House' in *The Scarlet Letter*, offers a deeply reflexive observation on the difference between fact in truth and fact in story-telling:

> We have a few old mouth-to-mouth tales; we exhume from old trunks and boxes and drawers letters without salutation or signature, in which men and women who once lived and breathed are now merely initials or nicknames out of some now incomprehensible affection which sound to us like Sanskrit or Chocktaw; we see dimly people, the people in whose living blood and seed we ourselves lay dormant and waiting, in this shadowy attenuation of time possessing now heroic proportions, performing their acts of simple passion and simple violence, impervious to time and inexplicable—Yes, Judith, Bon, Henry, Sutpen: all of them. They are there, yet something is missing; they are like a chemical formula exhumed along with the letters from that forgotten chest, carefully, the paper old and faded and falling to pieces, the writing faded, almost indecipherable, yet meaningful, familiar in shape and sense, the name and presence of volatile and sentient forces; you bring them together in the proportions called for, but nothing happens; you re-read, tedious and intent, poring, making sure that you have forgotten nothing, made no miscalculation; you bring them together again and again nothing happens: just the words, the symbols, the shapes themselves, shadowy inscrutable and serene, against that turgid background of a horrible and bloody mischancing of human affairs.

In terms albeit high Southern and florid, Mr. Compson intones what might pass as a modernist's credo, the inescapability of 'something missing' whenever human experience is pressed into narrative. Such a credo, we cannot doubt, lies close to Faulkner's own. Nonetheless, the story *does* get told, through to the shooting of Bon by Henry and to Sutpen's own decapitation with Wash Jones's scythe (later to be described as the 'symbolic laurel of a caesar's triumph'). We also experience it, as Mr. Compson indicates, in 'the proportions called for', as italicized snippets of interior monologue, as again letters, as efforts of personal recall and a search for connections. Each acts in alliance with, and in modification of, the other, essential parts in the whole yet none of necessity revealing more than the truth in part.

The novel moves formally to an end, in its last four chapters, by changing from the humidity and magnolia of

Modernist Faulkner? A Yoknapatawpha Trilogy

Mississippi to the iron cold of New England. It also moves from history as single witness to history as interrogation in the form of Quentin and Shreve. Again the litany of event is there to be discerned: Sutpen's 'innocence' in seeking to father a last son on Wash's granddaughter Milly, the discovery of the gravestones of Sutpen, Judith and Charles Etienne St. Valéry Bon, the rôle of Clytie in the Sutpen lives, the burning down of Sutpen's Mansion when, finally, Quentin does go 'out there' with Rosa to glimpse as some left-over shadow from an earlier epoch the figure of Henry Sutpen, and the last, mocking bewailment of Jim Bond over the burnt embers of the house.

But the energy which feeds the telling of these events lies elsewhere, in Shreve's urgent and fascinated concern to reconstitute the story and more generally to understand the South (' "What is it? something you live and breath in air" '), in the charade whereby he and Quentin play out the rôles of Henry and Bon, and in Quentin's spiralling love-hatred of his heritage (' "*I dont. I dont! I dont hate it! I dont hate it*" '). The ever faster exchanges of question and answer, with each accompanying call to explanation or patience, invite our witness as much to the motion of story-telling as of history. '*Maybe nothing ever happens once and is finished*', says Quentin. If so, *Absalom, Absalom!*, in common with most of the Yoknapatawpha fiction, supplies a style of telling to match. Faulkner indeed belongs in the modernist pantheon, but always with a certain reservation. Behind all the reflexivity, the self-reference, his fiction unmistakeably bears an older tradition in its train, the new as custodian of the old.

NOTES

1. Frederick L. Gwynn and Joseph L. Blotner (eds.), *Faulkner in the University: Class Conferences at the University of Virginia, 1957–1958*, (Charlottesville, Virginia: University of Virginia Press and Vintage Books, 1959), p. 239.
2. These and other biographical details are taken from: Joseph Blotner, *Faulkner: A Biography*, 2 vols (New York: Random House, 1974) and Frederick R. Karl, *William Faulkner: American Writer* (New York: Weidenfeld & Nicholson, 1989).

3. Blotner (op. cit.), p. 1344.
4. Blotner (op. cit.), p. 1364, Karl (op. cit.), p. 806. See also *New York Times*, 7 July 1962, 6.
5. A representative account of Faulkner's supposed failings would be: Norman Podhoretz, 'William Faulkner and the Problem of War', *Commentary*, XVIII, September 1954, 227–32.
6. Malcolm Cowley (ed.), *The Portable Faulkner* (New York: Viking Press, 1946). Reference, too, has to be made to Malcolm Cowley (ed.), *The Faulkner-Cowley File: Letters and Memories, 1944–1962* (New York: Viking Press, 1966).
7. See William Faulkner, 'Albert Camus', *Transatlantic Review*, Spring 1961. Reprinted in James B. Meriwether (ed.), *Essays, Speeches and Public Letters* by William Faulkner (New York: Random House), pp. 113–14.
8. Notably Jean-Paul Sartre, 'On *The Sound and the Fury*: Time in the Work of Faulkner'. Reprinted in Robert Penn Warren (ed.), *Faulkner: A Collection of Critical Essays* (Englewood Cliffs, New Jersey: Prentice-Hall, Inc., 1966).
9. All quotations from the novels are from the Modern Library/Random House editions as derived from the following first editions: *The Sound and the Fury* (New York: Jonathan Cape and Harrison Smith, 1929; Modern Library, 1946); *As I lay Dying* (New York: Cape and Smith, 1930; Modern Library, 1946); and *Absalom, Absalom!* (New York: Random House, 1936).
10. The critical literature on Faulkner is now voluminous, but I want especially to acknowledge the following studies: Frederick Hoffman and Olga Vickery (eds.), *William Faulkner: Three Decades of Criticism* (East Lancing: Michigan State University Press, 1960); Lawrance R. Thompson, *William Faulkner: An Introduction and Interpretation* (New York: Barnes and Noble, 1963); Robert Penn Warren (ed.), *Faulkner: A Collection of Critical Essays* (op. cit.); Richard P. Adams, *Faulkner: Myth and Motion* (Princeton, New Jersey: Princeton University Press, 1968; Linda W. Wagner (ed.), *William Faulkner: Four Decades of Criticism* (East Lancing: Michigan State University Press, 1973); André Bleikasten, *The Most Splendid Failure: Faulkner's 'The Sound and the Fury'* (Bloomington: University of Indiana Press, 1976); Arthur F. Kinney, *Faulkner's Narrative Poetics: Style as Vision* (Amherst: University of Massachusetts Press, 1978); David Minter, *William Faulkner: His Life and Work* (Baltimore: Johns Hopkins Press, 1980); Carolyn Porter, *Seeing and Being: The Plight of the Participant Observer in Emerson, James, Adams and Faulkner* (Middletown: Weslyan University Press, 1981); and Richard Brodhead (ed.), *Faulkner: New Perspectives* (Englewood Cliffs, New Jersey: Prentice-Hall, Inc., 1983).
11. *Faulkner in the University* (op. cit.), 15 February 1957, p. 1.
12. For a splendid recent account of this aspect of Faulkner, see Stephen M. Ross, *Fiction's Inexhaustible Voice: Speech and Writing in Faulkner* (Athens, Georgia: University of Georgia Press, 1989).
13. This and other stereotypes as they transfer to the screen are studied

Modernist Faulkner? A Yoknapatawpha Trilogy

   in Donald Bogle, *Toms, Coons, Mulattoes, Mammies and Bucks* (New York: Viking Press, 1973).
14. Jean Stein, 'William Faulkner: An Interview', *Paris Review*, Spring 1956. Reprinted in Frederick Hoffman and Olga W. Vickery (eds.), *William Faulkner: Three Decades of Criticism* (op. cit.).
15. *Faulkner in the University* (op. cit.), 15 April 1957, p. 87.
16. The phrase is taken from Herman Melville, *Mardi: A Voyage Thither* (1849).
17. *Faulkner in the University* (op. cit.), 8 May 1958, pp. 273–74.

3
Faulkner, Women and Yoknapatawpha: From Symbol to Autonomy

by FAITH PULLIN

'It's wrong to think about women as if they were dishonest men. They ain't. They're just women.'
—William Faulkner[1]

'If Venus returned she would be a soiled man in a subway lavatory with a palm full of French post-cards.'
—The Wild Palms[2]

'No bloody moon.'
—The Unvanquished[3]

From the adolescent romanticism of *Mosquitoes* (1927) to the sociological awareness of *The Mansion* (1959), Faulkner is engaged in a struggle to move from the conviction of woman as *other* to a sense of her as androgynous, or truly human. Linda Snopes Kohl frees herself from the bonds of a perversely gynocentric society and presents, in her own being and actions, an alternative version of southern society. In the words of the critic, Keith Louise Fulton, Kohl:

> walks out of the mansion and closes the door on the American dream of a patriarchal dynasty after achieving what no other

female or male character in Faulkner's fiction achieves, an act of justice that settles her conflicts with the past and empowers her move into the future.[4]

In *Mosquitoes*, an apprentice work, paying homage to Swinburne, Verlaine and Eliot, Faulkner sets his sexual agenda, creating a series of female stereotypes that, nevertheless, prefigure his more subtle later characterizations. Besides female sexual types, Faulkner also presents a variety of physical and sexual experiences—which include, as Blotner points out, 'masturbation, conception, constipation, evacuation, lesbianism, syphilis, and perversion'.[5] In spite of the gratuitously sensational nature of this material, it was clear from the start that Faulkner intended incorporating into his text new ways of perceiving women.

In an important essay published in 1978, Ilse Dusoir Lind, comments on his inclusion of biological data in his depictions of women: 'Like Whitman he saw through the drapery whether allowed to or not, thereby acknowledging the full physicality of woman, no less than that of man.'[6] Lind also adduces convincing circumstantial evidence that Faulkner was familiar with the work of Dr. Louis Berman whose *The Glands Regulating Personality* provided a medical interpretation of, for example, Joanna Burden's menopausal behaviour. Faulkner's problem was to incorporate the scientific evidence of Berman and Havelock Ellis into his representations of women existing within the confines of a conservative, phallocratic and racist society. In spite of the dictum of Dawson Fairchild (a version of Sherwood Arderson) that women are 'merely articulated genital organs with a kind of aptitude for spending whatever money you have', Faulkner follows Havelock Ellis (actually mentioned by name in *Mosquitoes*) in accepting the latent bisexuality of each sex. Consequently, Gordon 'examined with growing interest [Patricia's] flat breast and belly, her boy's body which the poise of it and the thinness of her arms belied'.[7]

The painter, Dorothy Jameson, herself unable to maintain reciprocal interest in, and from, men, contrasts her niece, Patricia, with Jenny whose frank sensuality is her greatest appeal: 'an utterly mindless rifeness of young, pink flesh, a supine potential fecundity lovely to look upon; a doll awaiting a quickening and challenging it with neither joy nor sorrow'.[8] The androgynous appeal of Patricia creates an obsessive fascination in Gordon and David West; she herself responds only to her brother who calls her 'Gus'. As Blotner has intimated, sex rôles and characteristics seem interchangeable here; Patricia's brother toys with Jenny 'in what seems a perfunctory manner', whereas Patricia demonstrates the 'mindless imitativeness and devotion of a younger brother for an older one'. *Mosquitoes*, then, raises the issues of bisexuality, incest, virginity, and presents, in Jenny, an early example of woman as archetype, 'the symbol of a desire'.

Faulkner's major female characters often present problems of interpretation because they exist in several dimensions, not necessarily closely integrated. Lena Grove in *Light in August* (1932) can be seen as some kind of visiting goddess of nature, arriving and departing without explanation, and at the same time as an inadequate, deprived personality who resolutely refuses to come to terms with reality. As has been noted by several critics, she remains defined by the community, unborn as a separate identity and served by men and women alike by reason of her biological imperative. In the same way, her obverse, Joanna Burden, though acting autonomously on one level, is, on another, merely the victim of the forces that have made her; her individuality consisting simply in her northern differences from the southern community which marginalizes her. Faulkner's own comment on Lena, 'She was the captain of her soul',[9] reveals a masculinist bias at odds with the actual text. No woman character in a Faulkner novel is the captain of her soul until the emancipation of Linda Snopes Kohl—a process itself enabled by the suicide of her mother. The society of *Light in August* is a harshly patriarchal one, limiting the possibilities of all women, and most deviant men (Hightower, Byron Bunch). The *locus* for its conflicts of gender and race is, of course, Joe Christmas himself whose indeterminate position in relation to masculinity/femininity, blackness/whiteness, is summed up in the phrase 'womanshenegro'. Christmas often takes the female rôle in relating to others, with Lucas Burch and with Joanna Burden. His own hatred of women comes from his complex

Faulkner, Women and Yoknapatawpha: From Symbol to Autonomy

internalization of his society's value system; because of his own ambiguous position, Joe responds with hatred to women in general—his revulsion expressed in statements like 'even a male horse is a kind of man.' In his presentation of Joe, Faulkner emphasizes the misogyny of southern society in order to criticize it. Joe is a case-study of great depth and subtlety in which Faulkner develops at length the rationale behind the anti-feminine assessments of many of his other male characters ('once a bitch always a bitch'). In this respect, Faulkner is in advance of his time in his perception of black women as at the lowest point in the social structure, the repository of all contempt. Joe's adolescent sexual initiation is deflected into physical violence because of his fear and revulsion for women and the female body:

> He kicked her hard, kicking into and through a choked wail of surprise and fear. She began to scream, he jerking her up, clutching her by the arm, hitting at her with wide, wild blows, striking at the voice perhaps, feeling her flesh anyway, enclosed by the womanshenegro and the haste.[10]

Joe's violent over-reactions to women, though socially sanctioned, indicate a profound fear of the feminine in himself: a fear ironically objectified in his death by castration in which he may be said to *become* a woman. Joe's early indoctrination by McEachern has meant that he identifies with the community's rigid values of will and self-assertion in opposition to feeling and co-operation. The purest version of this type is Percy Grimm, Joe's murderer, and described elsewhere by Faulkner as comparable to a Nazi Storm-trooper. For Faulkner, Joe's tragedy was that he did not know what he was:

> He deliberately evicted himself from the human race because he didn't know where he was. That was his tragedy, that to me was the tragic, central idea of the story—that he didn't know what he was, and there was no way possible in life for him to find out—which to me is the most tragic condition a man could find himself in—not to know what he is and to know that he will never know.[11]

Joe's problems of identity are not shared by Joanna Burden, but his rôle as victim is. As an unmarried female, Joanna has no status in a reactionary society, for she is not of the age at which Faulkner's Aunt Jennys become admirable and respected.

The repressed nature of the lives of white males in this culture means that spontaneity or any kind of unstructured response is projected onto women and makes them objects of fear. Consequently, Joe recognizes McEachern 'without surprise': 'Perhaps he was thinking then how he and the man could always count upon one another, depend upon one another; that it was the woman alone who was unpredictable.'[12]

Punishment itself is 'a natural and inescapable fact' which McEachern's wife sullies by 'getting in the way', by giving it 'an odor, an attenuation, and aftertaste'. Again, Faulkner significantly comments on the abstracted 'pure' impersonal nature of male interaction and society's imputation of the impure, the unclean to women.

Joanna Burden is as intense and complex in her psychic conflicts as Christmas himself; her situation as a New England exile in the south is crucial to her own view of herself and her social rôle in Jefferson; but, at the same time, she was born in and has lived in the same house all her life—a home which is and is not a home. Paradoxes and contradictions abound:

> she had never been away from Jefferson for a longer period than six months at any time and these only at wide intervals filled with homesickness for the sheer boards and nails, the earth and trees and shrubs, which composed the place which was a foreign land to her and her people.[13]

In Joanna, Faulkner presents 'womansuffering' in the Hawthornean sense of inherited sin. Joanna's father instructs her that she cannot escape 'the shadow': 'The curse of the black race is God's curse. But the curse of the white race is the black man who will be forever God's chosen own because He once cursed Him.'[14]

Joanna's representative destiny is to 'raise the black shadow' and to do it in a land where she will be hated and feared because of the subversive nature of that enterprise: 'stirring up the negroes to murder and rape, they called it. Threatening white supremacy.'[15]

Joanna is subversive of southern patriarchy in her sexual behaviour also. Unlike McEachern's wife, whose kindness Joe sees as tainted by 'a woman's affinity and instinct for secrecy, for casting a faint taint of evil about the most trivial and innocent actions', Joanna operates with the impersonality of the male. In their preliminary sexual encounter, Joe has to fight up to the final instant with her 'mantrained muscles and mantrained habit of thinking born of heritage and environment':

> There was no feminine vacillation, no coyness of obvious desire and intention to succumb at last. It was as if he struggled physically with another man for an object of no actual value to either, and for which they struggled on principle alone.[16]

Joanna's death is precipitated by her insistence that Joe becomes a suppliant to a white male God; he feels that he is merely instrumental in her death—a death which has always been an inevitability. He has to refuse to submit and refuse the association with blacks in order to support the concept of maleness; he kills her out of the same motivation that makes him refuse to marry her: 'No, if I give in now, I will deny all the thirty years that I have lived to make me what I chose to be.' Joanna's death is implicit in the logic of the narrative since she refuses to be categorized as 'female' and cannot be contained within any definition of southern womanhood. Similarly, Christmas explodes patriarchal and racial categories and causes Grimm to destroy him in the name of white supremacy. Grimm's final denunciation of Christmas links him with other marginalized outcasts of Jefferson:

> 'Jesus Christ!' Grimm cried, his young voice clear and outraged like that of a young priest. 'Has every preacher and old maid in Jefferson taken their pants down to the yellowbellied son of a bitch?'[17]

As Doreen Fowler has demonstrated, in her essay 'Joe Christmas and "Womanshenegro"',[18] the domination of white male values in Jefferson has a brutalizing effect on the sexual identities of women, causing them to deny their own natures: 'the roster of women in this category reads like a list of battle casualties.'

Heading the list is Mrs. McEachern 'a patient, beaten creature without sex demarcation at all save the neat screw of graying hair and the skirt' . . . Another sexually deformed creature is the 'woodenfaced,' 'dead voice[d]' Mrs. Hines, who, after having suffered her domineering husband's brawling 'two-fisted evangelism' for forty years, now also presents to the eye no sign of her gender 'save for the skirt which [she] wears'; yet another casualty of male power is Milly Hines, whose father, by ruling that no doctor will attend the delivery of her child, effectively consigns his own child to death.

Even relatively benign figures like Hightower refuse their wives the sensitive responses that they need in order to survive.

Faulkner ends *Light in August* with the narrative of the furniture repairer whose male view of Lena is of a subtly exploitative young woman who has decided that she likes travelling and 'had got along all right this far, with folks taking good care of her'. Faulkner himself spoke of his amusement at Lena's concluding words: 'My, my. A body does get around. Here we aint been coming from Alabama but two months, and now it's already Tennessee.' In so doing, he makes plain that the comic, celebratory note is to be the dominant one; but Lena remains a blank space in the text—a figure defined in the most generalized terms both by male characters and male author. She carries the positive values of the tale but exists principally as a counterweight to the in-depth investigation of Christmas's psyche. His dilemma focuses and privileges male concerns. Yet, at the same time, though treating his women characters as inevitably subsidiary, Faulkner interrogates what it is to be *male* or *female* in this caste-ridden society and indicates that different realities and recognitions are possible. In the words of Doreen Fowler: 'With Joe Christmas, Faulkner implies that male/female, black/white distinctions are not irreconcilable opposites, but rather only the opposing ends of one continuum.'[19] In reply to an undergraduate questioner, Faulkner said that it was much more fun to try to write about women than men and also much more difficult; he maintained that women are 'marvellous', 'wonderful' and, in addition, much stronger and much more determined than men. Such idealizations can arouse readerly suspicions. Estelle Faulkner tried to resolve queries about Faulkner's ambivalent attitudes when she reported that some people thought Faulkner hated women by the way he wrote about them. 'When someone asked me why he disliked them so, I said I wasn't aware that he did. I was scared he liked women a little too much.'

Several recent studies have shown the ways in which the insights of Nancy Chodorow's *The Reproduction of Mothering: Psychoanalysis and the Sociology of Gender* (1978) can be used to illuminate Faulkner's attitudes to mothers and children, and Noel Polk in his essay, 'The Dungeon Was Mother Herself', had closely analysed the oppressive and punitive nature of mother figures in Faulkner's fiction written from 1927–31. Closely associated with these concerns is the tenderness shown towards children in Faulkner's writing and the interest in the possibilities of nurturing male figures. Faulkner's devotion is sometimes focussed on the text itself, as in the 1956 interview with Jean Stein in which he says that, of all his work, *The Sound and the Fury* (1928) caused him the most grief and anguish,

> as the mother loves the child who became the thief or murderer more than the one who became the priest. . . . It's the book I feel tenderest towards. I couldn't leave it alone.

Faulkner defined the essence of this story as 'a tragedy of two lost women: Caddy and her daughter'. Caddy is lost in another sense also, that in which she is absent from the text. Yet, again and again, Faulkner emphasizes Caddy's central importance in the narrative:

> So I, who had never had a sister and was fated to lose my daughter in infancy, set out to make myself a beautiful and tragic little girl.[20]

> To me she was the beautiful one, she was my heart's darling. That's what I wrote the book about and I used the tools which seemed to me the proper tools to try to tell it, try to draw the picture of Caddy.[21]

Although Caddy and what she represents (the reader does not know what she *is*) are crucial, Faulkner's often quoted reason for not allowing Caddy to tell her own story is highly significant:

> because Caddy was still to me too beautiful and too moving to reduce her to telling what was going on, that it would be more passionate to see her through somebody else's eyes, I thought.[22]

The problem here is that those eyes are male; Caddy is, on one level, merely a figment of the various imaginations of her three brothers and 'Faulkner' himself. Dilsey, though described by Faulkner as 'one of my own favourite characters, because she is brave, courageous, generous, gentle and honest', seems incapacitated as an efficient commentator on Caddy since, as Philip M. Weinstein has noted, she merely 'fulfills a white fantasy of a black woman essentially at ease and functioning within a patriarchal world'.[23] It is Mr. Compson whose dialogue with Quentin sets up the parameters of a discourse about women against which Quentin himself analyses his *own* feelings for his sister (she is as foreign to him, as much a creature of his own fears and desires as Little Sister Death, the mysterious female child who accompanies him on his last day). Mr. Compson conceives of women as another species—'women so delicate so mysterious Father said. Delicate equilibrium of periodical filth between two moons balanced', and in another central statement, Mr. Compson observes, 'women have an affinity for evil for supplying whatever the evil lacks in itself for drawing it about them instinctively as you do bed-clothing in slumber.' However, Mr. Compson recognizes that men, not women, have invented the doctrine of virginity and hints at the possibility of male projection onto the concept 'woman'. The necessity for Caddy to be voiceless, deprived of any but reported speech in her own narrative, culminates in Faulkner's appendix where the librarian realizes that Dilsey did not want to recognize the photograph of Caddy with the Nazi officer because *'she knows Caddy doesn't want to be saved hasn't anything any more worth being saved for nothing worth being lost that she can lose.'*[24] In other words, Caddy's function as symbol of Compson idealism is over. Quentin effectively has destroyed Caddy through his need to idealize her and his attempt to 'isolate her out of the loud world'. Caddy is victimized by the inadequacies of her family and forced into a mothering rôle, her own needs unmet; Quentin, her daughter, is deprived in cruder ways, materially and emotionally, by Jason. Both women are trapped into deviant behaviour—their only means of feeling free and real—a doomed attempt to escape from the words of the men who control them.

If *The Sound and the Fury* examines the destructive force of male idealism, *As I Lay Dying* (1930) deals with a female character who demands more than ordinary experience from life and insists on a deeper vision. In this case, it is the woman who rejects life because she is unable to accept its limitations; the man survives and creates a comic resolution to the quest. Addie begins life as an isolated character with no familial context and makes herself into a wife and mother as a means of making contact with others; but her qualities of imagination mark her out from the community: she discovers that

> sin and love and fear are just sounds that people who never sinned nor loved nor feared have for what they never had and cannot have until they forget the words.[25]

Addie is a multidimensional figure; she carries out her social and maternal rôles but cannot be encompassed by them. Her disappointed idealism leads, like Quentin's, to death—she is frustrated, not only by the limitations of her environment, but by the limitations of life itself. Words are so divorced from meanings in her life and fulfilment so impossible to attain, that Addie experiences herself as dying long before her actual death. Nothing in her later life measures up to the promise of intense experience symbolized by the wild geese flying north in early spring. Addie does her duty by marrying Anse and producing children, but these experiences, even the intensity of her adulterous relationship with the Reverend Whitfield, are ultimately failures. Quotidian experience kills the spirit. Anse is 'dead' to real living:

> He did not know he was dead. I would lie by him in the dark, hearing the dark land talking of God's love and His beauty and His sin; hearing the dark voicelessness in which the words are the deeds, and the other words that are not deeds, that are just the gaps in people's lacks, coming down

like the cries of the geese out of the wild darkness in the old terrible nights, fumbling at the deeds like orphans to whom are pointed out in a crowd two faces and told, that is your father, your mother.[26]

Addie has a greater comprehension of her father's words than he had himself:

My father said that the reason for living is getting ready to stay dead. I knew at last what he meant and that he could not have known what he meant himself, because a man cannot know anything about cleaning up the house afterward.[27]

Jewel's birth effectively ends Addie's real life because it marks the end of her spiritual search to fuse her own response to a higher reality with the duties of ordinary life. As a result of her inability to compromise, Addie finally rejects her children as well as her husband. Her life has given her little genuine satisfaction, but, superficially, she has played a positive rôle. Addie's demanding idealism is contrasted with the response to experience of her daughter Dewey Dell. Dewey Dell takes over the mothering rôle in the interim between Addie's death and the appearance of the new Mrs. Bundren; abused both by Lafe and MacGowan, nevertheless, it is clear that she will cope with her pregnancy and will make a better adjustment to reality than her mother. In *As I Lay Dying*, Faulkner shows the ways in which the romantic vision is doomed to failure, yet in Addie he has created a forceful personality who dominates her family and the narrative.

As Sally Page has pointed out in her *Faulkner's Women*[28] Charlotte Rittenmeyer, the heroine of *The Wild Palms* (1939), has much in common with Addie Bundren; both characters have a high degree of sensitivity both to the limitations and the possibilities of life. Charlotte is an absolutist whose quest for intensity of emotion forces her to try to make a relationship with Harry that exists entirely on its own terms, for and in itself. As Adam Mars-Jones comments in his introduction to the novel, 'misogyny in Faulkner has the status of a back-handed compliment; and there's a lot of it about.'[29] Charlotte's physical suffering as the result of a botched abortion performed by Harry fills the opening section and symbolizes the negativity of a futile attempt to escape societal demands and negotiate a separate peace. Charlotte is under no illusions about the price to be paid ('the value of love is the sum of what you have to pay for it and any time you get it cheap you have cheated yourself'). Charlotte is one of the most developed of Faulkner's androgynous heroines. She takes the initiative in every respect; her will dictates the way the couple live:

> Listen: it's got to be all honeymoon, always. For ever and ever, until one of us dies. It can't be anything else. Either heaven, or hell: no comfortable safe peaceful purgatory between for you and me to wait in until good behavior or forbearance or shame or repentance overtakes us.[30]

In his *Paris Review* interview, Faulkner stated that Charlotte Rittenmeyer and Harry Wilbourne sacrificed everything for love, and then lost that. He also described the method of composition of the novel as of one 'counterpoint':

> I invented the other story, its complete antithesis, to use as counterpoint. And I did not write those two stories and then cut one into the other. I wrote them, as you read it, as the chapters.[31]

In glaring opposition to Charlotte, the pregnant woman in the *Old Man* narrative survives various disasters and gives birth successfully, albeit in horrific conditions and with the unwilling help of the tall convict whose famous last expletive 'Women—!' contains a good deal of the narrator's and Faulkner's ambivalence.

Charlotte appears compelled to pursue the idea of love with puritanical zeal ('They say love dies between two people. That's wrong. It doesn't die. It just leaves you, goes away, if you are not good enough, worthy enough'). Harry is merely an instrument in that search and is even at one point emasculated into writing pulp romantic fiction ('certainly there seems to be no limit to what I can invent on the theme of female sex troubles'). Yet Harry is clear that prioritizing love is impossible:

> It took us a long time, but man is resourceful and limitless in inventing too, and so we have got rid of love at last just as we have got rid of Christ.[32]

William Faulkner: The Yoknapatawpha Fiction

Paradoxically, although the women of Yoknapatawpha are imprisoned in a repressive social code, Charlotte creates her own prison of love. The escape from the bonds of family and society involves her own destruction. Here, Faulkner comes perilously close to the 'anatomy is destiny' argument; Charlotte is punished for her refusal to continue to procreate and for her rejection of the children she has already produced. Nevertheless, Faulkner gives full play to Charlotte's complex personality; she is a creator in the areas of love and sex. She is a fully aware, original character expressing both the male and female components of her nature.

The twenty years separating the publication of the revised version of *Sanctuary* (1931) from *Requiem for a Nun* (1951) allowed Faulkner to embark on an exercise in inter-texuality. *Requiem* answers the questions raised in the earlier text about the reasons for Temple Drake's behaviour. The kind of discourse employed in *Requiem* requires discussion of crucial problems of morality and the sexual behaviour of women that are pertinent to the entire Faulkner *oeuvre*.

In Temple, Faulkner provides another example of 'the natural female infallibility for the spontaneous comprehension of evil'. Other women characters who inhabit the narrative are set at fixed points on Horace Benbow's scale of morality: Aunt Jenny, representing integrity and wisdom, Belle and Little Belle, rampant sexuality/promiscuity.

Narcissa, the sister with whom Benbow has an abnormally intense relationship ('You're in love with your sister. What do the books call it? What sort of complex?'), operates a punitive and self-serving moral code, refusing to rescue Ruby Goodwin, the one woman who shows sacrificial love:

> Don't you see, this is my home, where I must spend the rest of my life. Where I was born. I dont care where else you go nor what you do. I dont care how many women you have nor who they are. But I cannot have my brother mixed up with a woman people are talking about.[33]

Narcissa is a useful example of the psychopathological effects of the southern women's internalization of male ideals of purity and chastity. The mystery of why Temple behaves as she does—refusing to escape from Miss Reba's brothel when it would be perfectly possible for her to do so—is explained by Temple herself in her own voice in *Requiem*. In *Sanctuary* the narrator presents the reader with a configuration in which the outward moral show simply offers a paradox. As the supposed 'bad' woman, Ruby actually highlights the behaviour of the corrupt Temple, who at first only *plays* at decadence and who when threatened falls back on the self-protective repetition of 'My father's a judge'. Ruby articulates this double-standard when she tells Temple: 'But you good women. Cheap sports. Giving nothing, then when you're caught. . . . Do you think you're meeting kids now? Kids that give a damn whether you like it or not?'[34] She does so again to Temple with: 'Nobody cares whether you are afraid or not. Afraid? You haven't the guts to be really afraid, anymore than you have to be in love.'[35] Horace Benbow, at least, understands Ruby's worth and situation, as when he tells his sister that Ruby 'has nothing, no one' and that she asks 'nothing of anyone except to be left alone, trying to make something of her life when all you sheltered chaste women—'. But to Narcissa Ruby remains the pariah, the 'street-walker' and 'murderer's woman'.[36]

After the rape, it is clear that Temple now classifies herself as 'bad', one of the alienated opposed to and by the dominant social group. This is the reason why she refuses to escape, to reach sanctuary, and merely avoids the eyes of a former school fellow ('He nearly saw me! . . . He was almost looking right at me! . . . He was coming right toward me! A boy. At school.'). The fact that Temple's father is a judge is no longer any security—quite the reverse—since he will now judge *her*.

Temple continues her rôle-playing at Miss Reba's, but she has changed parts, transferring from flirtatious adolescent to cheap whore. As Robert R. Moore points out:

> Faulkner's characterization of Temple in Memphis is straight out of a grade B movie. She becomes a cheap twenties flapper, swilling gin, chain smoking, drinking and dancing at a local speakeasy until she works herself into a frenzy of sexual desire with Red.[37]

This transformation is not as surprising as some critics assume; Temple has been rôle-playing all her life, responding to the demands of southern society with its rigid systems of female behaviour. Anne Jones's *Tomorrow is Another Day* provides helpful clarification concerning the way southern women saw themselves:

> In Jones's opinion, the demands of the cult caused the Southern woman to become alienated from herself because the ideals to which she was expected to conform did not come from within herself; rather, they were socially imposed from without, evolved within the society to serve its special needs as a racist culture. As a consequence, the Southern woman tended to experience a psychic split. On the one hand, she often felt hypocritical while fulfilling her rôle. On the other, because she internalized these rôle expectations at deep levels, she often felt ashamed of herself as a natural woman. Aspiring to be as pure as the marble statue to which she was often compared, she still knew that her innermost thoughts and desires showed her to be merely human. Citing a recent study of diaries kept by Southern women Jones shows how they repeatedly accused themselves of being dishonest when they acted as their culture demanded and also guilty about their 'animal' nature, often likening the mind of a woman to a 'cage of unclean beasts.'[38]

On this analysis, the punitive attitude of Narcissa to Ruby is easily understandable.

Temple's alienation from herself is clearly evident in the 'bright, chatty monologue manner' in which she describes to Horace the circumstances of the rape:

> She went on like that, in one of those bright, chatty monologues which women can carry on when they realize that they have the centre of the stage; suddenly Horace realized that she was recounting the experience with actual pride, a sort of naive and impersonal vanity, as though she were making it up.

Significantly, Temple comments on her attempts to avoid the inescapable fact of her womanhood, her status as sexual object—imagining herself as a boy, or a 45-year-old schoolteacher with grey hair and spectacles, or an old man with a long white beard.

Miss Reba is aware of Temple's self-destructiveness ('She'll be dead, or in the asylum in a year, way him and her go on up there in that room') but unaware of the extent to which

Temple is acting out her version of a socially determined rôle. In the courtroom scene, Temple behaves like an automaton, the 'ruined, defenceless child'; deliberately but, at the same time, willessly she condemns an innocent man. In *Requiem for a Nun*, Faulkner seeks to account for this gross betrayal.

On finishing *Sanctuary*, Faulkner as reported by Blotner

> began to think what would be the future of that girl? and then I thought, What could a marriage come to which was founded on the vanity of a weak man? What would be the outcome of that? And suddenly that seemed to me dramatic and worthwhile.

In October 1933, Faulkner wrote to Hall Smith: 'I have . . . a good title, I think: REQUIEM FOR A NUN. It will be about a nigger woman. It will be a little on the esoteric side, like AS I LAY DYING.'[40]

Although superficially *Requiem* would seem to focus on another of Faulkner's sacrificially redemptive black women and Nancy Mannigoe ('a drunkard, a casual prostitute') is certainly one of the dispossessed, the text actually proposes a series of analytic dialogues between Temple Drake and Mrs. Gowan Stevens and between the writer and his text. *Requiem* and *Sanctuary* are intertexual and self-reflexive to an unusually high degree. Speaking of herself in the third person, Temple reveals why she had to have a 'dope-fiend whore' to talk to

> Temple Drake, the white woman, the all-Mississippi debutante, descendant of long lines of statesman and soldiers high and proud in the high proud annals of our sovereign state, couldn't find anybody except a nigger dope-fiend whore that could speak her language.

The reason was that

> Temple Drake liked evil. She only went to the ball game because she would have to get on a train to do it, so that she could slip off the train the first time it stopped, and get into the car to drive a hundred miles with a man.

Again, at Miss Reba's, 'I could have climbed down the rainspout at any time, the only difference being that I didn't.' Temple reveals what she believes to be her essential self when she explains her motivation—her love for Alabama Red. The letters she wrote to him were 'better than you would expect from a 17-year-old amateur:

> I mean, you would have wondered how anybody just seventeen and not even through freshman college, could have learned the—right words. Though all you would have needed probably would be an old dictionary from back in Shakespeare's time when, so they say, people hadn't learned how to blush at words.[42]

The death of Red has been called 'the most passionately erotic epistolary situation' in Faulkner's fiction:

> where Temple Drake's lover, Red, summoned to Miss Reba's by Temple's letters, is shot at the moment, as Temple says, 'when all of him except just his body was already in the room with me and the door locked at last for just the two of us alone.'[43]

This forbidden love shows Temple stripped bare of social rôles and expectations and aligns her with Ruby in *Sanctuary*. Mrs. Gowan Stevens looks back on Temple Drake and treats her authentic passion with sardonic detachment when she speaks of herself and Nancy Mannigoe as 'two sisters in sin swapping trade or anyway avocational secrets over Coca-Colas in the quiet kitchen'. Both women, Temple and Nancy her alter-ego, are positioned by Faulkner and his society in a place where they must bear moral guilt and it is guilt intimately related to sex. Nancy's killing of Temple's second child means that there will be no end to the guilt, not self-inflicted but inflicted on them both by the repressive codes of a patriarchal society.

Faulkner's trilogy, *The Hamlet* (1940), *The Town* (1957) and *The Mansion* (1959), shows in microcosm the developing emancipation of his female characters from patriarchal and mythological bonds. At her first introduction in *The Hamlet*, Eula Varner is:

> a soft ample girl with definite breasts even at thirteen and eyes like cloudy hothouse grapes and a full damp mouth always slightly open, [sitting] at her place in a kind of sullen bemusement of rife young female flesh.[44]

Eula exists, not as a person but as a male fantasy of perpetual fertility:

> her entire appearance suggested some symbology out of the old Dionysic times—honey in sunlight and bursting grapes, the writhen bleeding of the crushed fecundated vine beneath the hard rapacious trampling goat-hoof. She seemed to be not a living integer of her contemporary scene, but rather to exist in a teeming vacuum in which her days followed one another as though behind sound-proof glass, where she seemed to listen in sullen bemusement, with a weary wisdom heired of all mammalian maturity, to the enlarging of her own organs.[45]

This comic exuberance of description gives way to pain when Eula Varner is transformed into Mrs. Flem Snopes:

> The beautiful face did not even turn as the surrey drew abreast of the store. It passed in profile, calm, oblivious, incurious. It was not a tragic face: it was just damned.[46]

Later still, Eula becomes part of myth, remote and characterless:

> It was Flem Snopes' wife. She was in a white garment; the heavy braided club of her hair looked almost black against it. She did not lean out, she merely stood there, full in the moon, apparently blank-eyed or certainly not looking downward at them—the heavy gold hair, the mask not tragic and perhaps not even doomed: just damned.[47]

In her first secret interview with Gavin Stevens, though literally cut down to size (*'Why, she can't possibly be this small, this little'*), Eula speaks and acts for the first time in a decisive manner ('I don't like unhappy people. They're a nuisance.' 'Lock the door. I've already drawn the shade. Stop being afraid of things' . . .). Eula becomes ever more self-directed and purposeful in her effort to save Linda from the machinations of Snopes. As she says to Stevens: 'You don't know much about women, do you? Women aren't interested in poets' dreams. They are interested in facts.' According to Stevens, even Eula's relationship with Manfred de Spain is to an extent self-induced—'She was seduced simply by herself.'

Faulkner clearly felt a special affection for *The Town* and its central female protagonists: 'I still think it is funny, and at the end very moving; two women characters I am proud of.' And in a letter to Jean Stein he wrote: 'Just finishing the book. It breaks my heart. I wrote one scene and almost cried. I thought it was just a funny book but I was wrong.'[48] Eula Snopes's suicide elevates her to a dimension of heroism, far removed from the facile, mythological references with which she is associated when the reader first encounters her. The pathos of her unfilled life gives her considerable dignity:

> She was bored. She loved, had a capacity to love, for love, to give and accept love. Only she tried twice and failed twice to find somebody not just strong enough to deserve, earn it, match it, but even brave enough to accept it.[49]

Linda Snopes is physically less impressive than her mother —certainly more androgynous—but has even more determined integrity. Freeing herself from the South, taking part in a foreign war, stoically enduring physical injury and humiliation and returning to take revenge on her father, Linda is comparable to the heroines of classical tragedy. Hardened by her experiences of war and work and by bereavement, Linda Snopes Kohl is Faulkner's least ambivalent female character. Her very appearance is at the other extreme from her mother's gender—coded allure:

> she dressed as usual in the clothes she seemd to spend most of her time walking about the adjacent countryside in—the expensive English brogues scuffed and scarred but always neatly polished each morning, with wool stockings or socks beneath worn flannel trousers or a skirt or sometimes what looked like a khaki boiler-suit under a man's stained burberry; this in the fall and winter and spring; in the summer it would be cotton-dress or skirt or trousers, her head with its single white plume bare even in the worst weather.[50]

In refusing all easy options and taking on the burden of personhood, Linda Snopes Kohl resolves male/female contradictions and concludes Faulkner's fictive analysis of gender relations. *The Mansion* privileges self-realization for women, and, at the same time, suggests new possibilities for American society.

Faulkner, Women and Yoknapatawpha: From Symbol to Autonomy

NOTES

1. Quoted by Joseph Blotner, 'William Faulkner: Life and Art', in *Faulkner and Women*, edited by Doreen Fowler and Ann. J. Abadie (University Press of Mississippi, 1986), p. 18.
2. *The Wild Palms* (Penguin Modern Classics, 1987), p. 98.
3. *The Unvanquished* (Penguin Modern Classics, 1988), p. 170. I follow Winifred Frazer in her suggestion that 'no bloody moon' really means 'no bloody woman' ('Faulkner and Womankind' in *Faulkner and Women*).
4. Keith Louise Fulton, 'Linda Snopes Kohl: Faulkner's Radical Woman', *Modern Fiction Studies, Feminism and Modern Fiction*, Autumn 1988, Vol. 34, No. 3, 425–36.
5. Joseph Blotner, *Faulkner: A Biography* (Random House, 1974), p. 514.
6. 'Faulkner's Women' in *The Maker and the Myth*, edited by Evans Harrington and Ann J. Abadie (University Press of Mississippi, 1978), p. 93.
7. *Mosquitoes*, (Chatto and Windus, 1964), p. 26.
8. Ibid., p. 89.
9. *Lion in the Garden: Interviews with William Faulkner, 1926–1962*, edited by James B. Meriwether and Michael Millgate (Random House, 1968), p. 253.
10. *Light in August* (Chatto and Windus, 1968), p. 147.
11. *Faulkner in the University*, edited by F. Gwynn and J. Blotner, p. 31–2.
12. *Light in August*, p. 149.
13. Ibid., p. 227.
14. Ibid., p. 240.
15. Ibid., p. 235.
16. Ibid., p. 222.
17. Ibid., p. 439.
18. *Faulkner and Women*, p. 149–50.
19. 'Joe Christmas and "Womanshenegro" ' in *Faulkner and Women*, p. 159.
20. Quoted by Michael Millgate in *The Achievement of William Faulkner* (Random House, 1963), p. 26.
21. Faulkner in the University, p. 6, *Class Conferences at the University of Virginia, 1957–1958* (University of Virginia Press, 1959).
22. Ibid., p. 1.
23. 'Faulkner's Rendering of Women' in *Faulkner and Women*, p. 85.
24. *The Portable Faulkner*, edited by Malcolm Cowley (Penguin, 1987), p. 716.
25. *As I Lay Dying* (Penguin Modern Classics, 1975), p. 138.
26. Ibid.
27. Ibid., p. 139.
28. Chapter 6, *The Female Idealist: As I Lay Dying and The Wild Palms*, p. 111.
29. *The Wild Palms*, vii–viii.

30. Ibid., p. 61.
31. *Lion in the Garden*, p. 132.
32. *The Wild Palms*, p. 98.
33. *Sanctuary* (Picador Classics, 1989), p. 129.
34. Ibid., p. 42–3.
35. Ibid., p. 45.
36. Ibid., p. 81.
37. 'Temple Drake's Self-Victimization' in *Faulkner and Women*, p. 123.
38. Quoted by Ilse Dusoir Lind, 'Faulkner Studies and Women's Studies' in *Faulkner and Women*, p. 29–30.
39. *Sanctuary*, p. 151.
40. Joseph Blotner, *Faulkner: A Biography* (Random House, 1974), p. 1313–14.
41. *Requiem for a Nun* (Penguin Modern Classics, 1987), p. 105.
42. Ibid., p. 128–29.
43. James G. Watson, ' "But Damn Letters Anyway": Letters and Fictions' in *New Directions in Faulkner Studies*, edited by Doreen Fowler and Ann J. Abadie (University Press of Mississippi, 1984), p. 239.
44. *The Hamlet* (Random House, 1931), p. 10.
45. Ibid., p. 95.
46. Ibid., p. 270.
47. Ibid., p. 311.
48. Blotner, pp. 1613, 359.
49. *The Town* (Random House, 1957), p. 359.
50. *The Mansion* (Random House, 1959), p. 362.

4

Law, Justice and Justification in William Faulkner

by ERIC MOTTRAM

1

In August 1955 William Faulkner told students at Nagano that he read Joseph Conrad 'regularly'.[1] And it is indeed clear that he shares many of Conrad's convictions about the forms of control to which human beings are always subject—convictions which he also recognized in Thomas Hardy and in Ernest Hemingway, the latter whose formulation is cited explicitly in *Requiem for a Nun*. These men need to believe in a process within which decisions in law and justice are never specifically human. Conrad's universe in 1897, for instance, is a machine which has evolved itself:

> out of a chaos of scraps of iron and behold!—it knits. I am horrified at the horrible work and stand appalled. . . . The infamous thing has made itself: made itself without thought, without conscience, without foresight . . . without heart. It is a tragic accident, and it has happened. You can't interfere with it. . . . It has knitted time, space, pain, death, corruption, despair, and all the illusions,—and nothing matters.[2]

Hardy wrote to Edward Wright:

> The will of man is neither wholly free, nor wholly unfree. When swayed by the Universal Will (which he mostly must be as a subservient part of it) he is not individually free; but

whenever it happens that all the rest of the Great Will is in equilibrium the minute portion called one person's will is free.

Max Beerbohm parodies Hardy in 'A Sequelula to *The Dynasts*':

> Let's lay down no laws to trip up on,
> Our way is in darkness,
> And not but by groping unhampered
> We win to the light. . . .

But a determinist plot for explanatory stories of resistance and endurance easily outplays parody. Faulkner's law and justice erode in this entropic plot, and his large sentences are time units trying to resist truths of plot by the arts of story. Gowrie law and mob justice in *Intruder in the Dust* insert rules of injustice into court order. The pattern persists in some of the most popular films of the late twentieth century, for example the westerns of Clint Eastwood. But all society's members contribute to crime. In *Light in August*, the K.K.K. beat Hightower unconscious within precisely these insertions and contributions. Order is marginalized. A sense of injustice may result in lynching or castration—the fate of Joe Christmas and of the heroes of Tennessee Williams's *Orpheus Descending* and *Sweet Bird of Youth*.

Alfred Kazin's essay 'The Stillness in *Light in August*' long ago recognized the 'complicity' of society in the making and breaking of obedience and disobedience; and Faulkner certainly read Hemingway's attributions of power to 'they' in *A Farewell to Arms* as elsewhere, the irresistible play and social force of what Hardy calls the Great Will. The citizens of Jefferson could not prevent the Snopes accession, nor could they absolutely condemn or absolutely uphold the murder of Flem at the end of *The Mansion*. At the beginning of *The Wild Palms* (1939) 'outrage' inherits a key Faulkner term for the existential absurd and is directed at the trap which fuses legal force and their own wills into 'the force and power of blind and visible Motion'. For the first convict, outrage is

> directed not at the men who have foiled his crime, not even at the lawyers and judges who had sent him here, but at the writers, the uncorporeal names attached to the stories, the paper novels—the Diamond Dicks and Jesse Jameses and

such—whom he believed had led him into this present predicament through their own ignorance and gullibility
and the 'criminal' impracticability of their behaviour and beliefs. After two years analysing the stories and methods, and 'peddling . . . subscriptions to the *Detectives' Gazette*' to obtain the required black handkerchief, dark lantern and pistol, he is simply immediately arrested.

For the second convict, outrage is directed not at the complicity of printed fiction but at 'the paradoxical fact that he had been forced to come here of his own free choice . . . between the Mississippi State penal farm and the Federal Penitentiary at Atlanta'. The 'vicious and fabulous quality' of his 199 years sentence precisely indicates the ambivalence and impotence of human legal administrations within the knitting machine:

> the very men, the paladins and pillars of justice and equity who have sent him here had during that moment become blind apostles not of mere justice but of all human decency, blind instruments not of equity but of all human outrage and vengeance, acting in a savage personal concert, judge, lawyer and jury, which certainly abrogated justice and possibly even law. Possibly only the Federal State's Attorney knew what the crime actually was. . . .

But Harry Wilbourne, the abortionist interne, and the convict join the long roll of Faulkner's jailed—Mink Snopes in Parchman penitentiary, Nancy Mannigoe in Jefferson, the Corporal, Lucas Birch and Joe Christmas, Boon Hogganbeck, Lucas Beauchamp, Samuel Warsham (in *Go Down, Moses*), Lee Goodwin in *Sanctuary*)—and Temple Drake imprisoned in a Memphis brothel, and Benjy and Darl enclosed in mental asylums for their madness. The absurd epitome is the problematic self-regard of Popeye before hanging. As the noose breaks his 'sleek, oiled . . . hair loose', with his hands tied he tries to jerk his hair back into place, and then attracts the sheriff-hangman's attention:

> The sheriff looked at him; he quit jerking his neck and stood rigid, as though he had an egg balanced on his head. 'Fix my hair, Jack,' he said.
> 'Sure,' the sheriff said. 'I'll fix it for you', springing the trap.

So justice ends in a joke.

William Faulkner: The Yoknapatawpha Fiction

Cut to Temple Drake and her judge father in the deathly isolation of the Luxembourg Gardens. In 'Pantaloon in Black' the sheriffs again have their problems, balancing between rough justice—lynch-law against 'niggers'—and the statuary law they are elected to enforce. But their complex sense of being representative citizens includes being elected to allow lynch-law when the primitive time is appropriate. The Warden has to obey law against his own sense of equity: 'It's hard luck. I'm sorry.' To which the convict of the 'Old Man' part of *The Wild Palms* replies: 'All right. If that's the rule.' No trial. The trial in *Sanctuary* again involves inherited community interactions between kinds of rule. Horace Benbow, weak and complicit lawyer for Goodwin's defence, vomits uncontrollably. In the enclosures of law, hypocrisy is commonplace, except in the most depraved of the depressed classes. Justice is as accidental as equity. Sadism penetrates the social scene, as if Popeye were its radiating centre. Kidnapped into a brothel, the imprisoned Temple Drake realizes her own sexuality—she is 17—and the resulting scepticism about choice and force is as penetrating as it is in *The Wild Palms*; ambivalent law and justice in fact penetrate their unfinished business through to Temple's children in *Requiem for a Nun*. But this sexual penetration of the legal is part of what, in *The Hamlet*, is called 'the old Dionysic times', 'the written bleeding of the crushed fecundated vine beneath the hard rapacious trampling goat-hoof', only too near an idiot's impulsive existence and, for Faulkner, explicitly an origin at the beginnings of western 'tragedy'.

The human violations in Greek tragedies occur within an appalling stasis controlled by fates and gods, and the dramatic actions are sacrificial to the ambivalences of the god of uncontrollable and blind energies, Dionysus. Although the goat-god's alter ego, the phallic assertions, were paraded at the conclusion of the tragedy event, the sense of enclosure remained. As early as 1919, in the poems of *The Marble Faun* (1924)—Hawthorne's title in 1860—a sense of human enclosure and nature's freedom is emphatic:

> The sky
> Warms me and yet I cannot break
> My marble bonds. That quick snake

> Is free to come and go, while I
> Am prisoner to dream and sigh
> For things I know, yet cannot know,
> 'Twixt sky above and earth below.

Elsewhere the faun exists under a spell within natural order, in a condition of suicidal inertia for 'a sad, bound prisoner'. The control is Pan—one of Dionysus's several names—making his pipe music, his art, within the cold stasis. In *A Green Bough*, published two years after *Sanctuary*, and six before *The Wild Palms*, the initial stasis is erotic—'a bullet through my heart' and the force of a sensuous woman robed in a crimson 'icy flame'—and moves into 'a furious emptiness of strife'. The hero appears as 'a terrific figure on an urn' in a Keatsian 'forgetting that he can't return'. Poem XVII addresses Atthis, changed into a fir-tree by a vengeful goddess,[3] with suicidal desire. There are, too, poems of hatred for the perpetual growth of nature, the uselessness of Spring, hatred of love, and restlessness without love, of Lilith as an entombed figure with whom human life must come to terms. The snake is now the Eden snake, already edging towards the serpent Ike McCaslin experiences in the Yoknapatawpha forests. What appear to be poems of personal anguish and imprisonment are part of continuing materials in Faulkner's fictions and their conditions of immutability, of laws limiting human resistance and change.

And while reading these poems, it might be useful to glance briefly at some curious features in Faulkner's 1925 sketches for the New Orleans' *Times—Picayune* and the *Double Dealer*.[4] In 'The Cop', he recalls leading a noisy nuisance life when a boy, but really wanting to be a law-enforcement agent:

> I would be a patrolman; in a blue coat and swinging a casual stick and with a silver shield on my breast, I would pace the streets away, with the measured beat of my footsteps . . . to be looked upon with respect by even grown people; to be the personification of bravery and the despair of criminals; to have a real pistol in my pocket!

The image remains into adolescence—'huge, calm, negligently talking with admiring girls . . . foiling the murderer, shooting him dead in the spitting darkness'. Even as a man

> sometimes pacing the dark empty streets, he wakes and I am briefly troubled over the futile bargain a man makes when he exchanges a small body and a great heart for a large body and hardly any heart at all; but not for long. Certainly man does not ever get what he wants in this world. . . . Anyway, I prefer to believe that this creature confronting the world bravely in a blue coat and a silver shield is quite a fellow, after all.

And there is one tale of a crutched man crying out to the cops: 'Arrest me! Where's laws and justice? Ain't I a member of the greatest republic on earth? . . . I got no gun; can't shoot you if I wanted. Come in and arrest me!' A third tale that looks forward into Faulkner's career tells of a bootlegger's discovery of a New Haven cop—one not previously 'fixed'. The judge would not be moved. But his colleague has fixed a deputy guarding the liquor to get him an airplane for escape—for $1,000. The flight is pretty risky, and the pilot and his deputy turn out to be the judge's twin sons. . . .

Requiem for a Nun (1951) places Temple Drake in the effects of her brothel experience and her erotic compromises with law and the court, eight years after *Sanctuary*. In the latter, Temple, now Mrs. Gowan Stevens, refuses to testify against Popeye and falsely accuses Lee Goodwin of a murder as well as rape. The mob take Goodwin from prison and burn him to death. In 1951 Faulkner needs to place this action—necessarily very briefly summarized here—within a history of Jefferson settlement, as part of the United States and not in a restriction called 'the South'. So the characters become exemplary (it is futile and mistaken for certain critics to accuse Faulkner of 'weakness' in using 'two-dimensional' and 'allegorical' figures). The condition is that there is no sanctuary, no sacred temple, no pure Southern belle, no automatic legal system or justice, no escape from law, no secure reliance on law, no automatically secure family (or marriage, legalized sexuality). Benbow earlier achieves a limited understanding of these facts. Now Gavin Stevens is the lawyer, and has learned his ambivalent situation from the beginning of his career, and certainly in *Intruder in the Dust* (1948)—that law invariably collides with forms of justice. Faulkner creates Temple Drake not as a 'sexist' example of his absurdly alleged belief that 'the only way to eliminate conflict is to eliminate women',[5] but to hold the key story that dramatizes the conditions of human ambivalences under law. *Requiem for a Nun* begins therefore—as *The Scarlet Letter* does—with settlement records: in this case, documents in the courthouse—'the simple dispossession of the Indians', 'the normal litter of man's ramshackle confederation against environment—that time and that wilderness', 'land grants and patents and transfers and deeds', 'bills of sale for slaves'. And as in *The Scarlet Letter* again, it is the jail which immediately signifies ambivalent transgression. History is given as the story of legal details and their signifying objects—the lock itself is 'the ancient Carolina lock from the last Nashville mail-pouch—the iron monster weighing almost fifteen pounds, with a key almost as long as a bayonet'. The courthouse 'hub' is embedded with Jefferson families, and therefore includes the insecure defence lawyer, Stevens, 'descendant of one of the pioneer Yoknapatawpha Families'. In the trial of Nancy Mannigoe, a Negro woman whose surname inherits 'Maingault' (in her 'heritage—or anyway patronym—runs Norman blood'), Stevens appears as:

> champion not so much of truth as of justice, or of justice as he sees it, constantly involving himself, often for no pay, in affairs of equity and passion and even crime too among his people, white and Negro both, sometimes directly contrary to his office of County Attorney which he has held for years, as is the present business.

Nancy herself represents intense, simplified belief in a force of equity beyond the human, and—in Stevens's words to Temple Drake—exemplifies 'that all human beings really don't stink'. She smothers Temple's baby to protect it from a criminal erotic life in Memphis. Temple discovers, therefore, that vengeance desires erode, since she cannot 'sacrifice a human life for it, even a nigger whore's'. Here, Faulkner inserts sacrifice as a social fact within the processes of law and justice, deeply implicated in all community and personal levels—as Goodwin's mob burning witnessed in *Sanctuary*. He has Stevens say: 'What we are trying to deal with

now is injustice. Only truth can cope with that or love.'
So the courthouse exemplifies complexities of attempts to
administer equity through law and justice at the interception
point of truth and love, and within the history of settlement
by possessiveness and individualism, frequently by violation.
The early settler left his descendant: 'scriptureless now and
armed only with the highwayman's, the murderer's pistol',
although the towns may be 'peopled by men with mouths
full of law'. Both law and outlawry are man-made and
man-destroyed: 'men's mouths were full of law and order,
all men's mouths round with the sound of money . . .
profit plus regimen equals security: a nation of common-
wealths.'

The 1903 Capitol, centre of government, which Stevens
and Temple visit to appeal Nancy's sentence into a pardon,
is a centre of impossibility:

> that gilded pustule, that Idea risen now, suspended like a
> balloon or a portent or a thundercloud above what used to be
> wilderness . . . triumvirate in legislative, judiciary, executive
> . . . the golden dome, the knob, the gleamy crumb . . . longer
> than a miasma and the gigantic ephemeral saurians. . . .

The present case cannot escape this story. Mrs. Temple
Stevens hired Nancy for someone to talk to commensurate
with her Memphis experience, but the latter discovered that
she planned to resist blackmail from her lover's brother not
by paying him off but by going away with him and taking
her baby daughter with her. Nancy saves the child by killing
her. 'Evil and corruption' are immediately once again a
complex issue. This is where Faulkner introduces Hemingway's existential stoicism—through Temple's memory of
it—and it proves to be the moral core of the plot and
its story:

> It's not that you must never even look on evil and corruption;
> sometimes you can't help that, you are not always warned.
> It's not even that you must resist it always. Because you've
> got to start much sooner than that. You've got to be prepared
> to resist it . . . you must have already said no to it before you
> even know what it is. . . .
>
> At first you think you can bear only so much and then you
> will be free. Then you find out that you can bear anything,

you really can and then it won't even matter. . . . All you have got to do is, refuse to accept. . . . Only, you have got to be told truthfully beforehand what you must refuse; the gods owe you that—at least a clear picture and a clear choice.

But, in Hemingway's terms in *A Farewell to Arms*—not directly quoted here:

> If people bring so much courage to this world the world has to kill them to break them, so of course it kills them. The world breaks every one and afterward many are strong at the broken places. But those that will not break it kills. It kills the very good and the very gentle and the very brave impartially. If you are none of these you can be sure it will kill you too but there will be no special hurry.[6]

Deleuze and Guattari ascribe this to the system of endless debt to the gods and the fathers that the West imposes on itself, at least since the Oedipus story, and certainly since the Christians, not to speak of Freud.[7] In Faulkner's terms: 'a promissory note with a trick clause . . . fate or luck or chance can foreclose on you without warning.' The baby girl's 'tender and defenceless innocence' is a cause for sacrifice. When the Christian god stated:

> 'Suffer little children to come unto Me', He meant suffer; that the adults, the fathers, the old in and capable of sin, must be ready and willing—nay, eager—to suffer at any time, that little children shall come unto Him unanguished, unterrified, undefiled.

Nancy enables just this. By that law, she is not guilty. Or rather, her plea is 'Yes, Lord, I done it.' The mockery of law is that Stevens has to coach her to plea 'Not Guilty' so that she can be sentenced to death. But then she says: 'Guilty, Lord', and wrecks the system:

> disrupting and confounding and dispersing and flinging back two thousand years, the whole edifice of corpus juris and rules of evidence we have been working to make stand up by itself ever since Caesar.

To the court, Nancy's plea 'had nothing to do with truth, only with law', and at the Capitol the governor cannot talk of justice only about 'a child', and in the language of legal apologetics:

> Who am I, to have the brazen temerity and hardihood to set the puny appanage of my office in the balance against that simple undeviable aim? Who am I, to render null and abrogate the purchase she made with that poor crazed lost and worthless life?

Faulkner follows with a long list of legal, quasi-legal and illegal examples of settlement, in long processual paragraphs that hold the story in its historicity, and bringing into it his own fictions of Yoknapatawpha. After the courthouse is gutted by Federal troops—but not the jail—

> a courthouse and city hall gang . . . every three or four years would try again to raze the old courthouse in order to build a new one . . . because the new one would bring the town and county that much more increment of unearned federal money.

By 1951 it is, even more devastatingly, the sign of 'one nation: no longer anywhere'. The jail also becomes morally iconic, and here two of Faulkner's forms of stasis reappear: it is 'older than album and stereopticon'—and 'Lilith's lost and insatiable face drawing the substance—the will and hope and dream and imagination—of all men . . . into that one bright fragile net and snare'. Inside law and justice are stereoptic stasis, the problems of forgiveness and salvation, sexual needs, urges to survive at all costs—the energies and inertias of settlement and individual endurance, which were Faulkner's perpetual combinatory controls.

In *The Wild Palms,* Wilbourne refuses to jump bail and, after sentencing to Parchman Penitentiary, refuses Rittenmayer's cyanide tablet. The public roar 'Kill him!'—and referring to him and his lover, Charlotte Rittenmayer, 'Hang them both! Lock them up together! Let the son of a bitch work on him this time with a knife!' Faulkner has Welbourne, in his cell, attempt to bring the events into timeless coherence, so that, in Hemingway's sense, they may become at least tolerable. Memory has to be made into story and history—which is exactly the function of Faulkner's fiction. Welbourne tries to statify the story into 'all of it':

Law, Justice and Justification in William Faulkner

> *Surely memory exists independent of the flesh.* But this was wrong too. *Because it wouldn't know it was memory,* he thought. *It wouldn't know what it was it remembered.*
> This was the second time he almost got it. But it escaped him. . . .

His appointed lawyer, Gower, just states his guilt. Once again, no trial. Wilbourne tries again—to understand how sexual love reaches court and sentence:

> *But it must be somewhere,* he thought. *There's the waste. Not just me . . . Let it be anyone. . . .* It seemed so little, so little to want, to ask. *With all the old graveyard-creeping, the old wrinkled, withered defeated clinging not even to the defeat but just to the habit. . . . So it is the old meat after all, no matter how old.* Because if memory *exists outside of the flesh it won't be memory because it won't know what it remembers so when she became not then half of memory became not and if I become not then all of memory will cease to be.*—Yes, he thought, *between grief and nothing I will take grief.*

So he chooses living, in prison. At the University of Virginia, in 1957, in reply to a question on *The Wild Palms*, Faulkner replied that, yes, he always favoured 'the individual rather than an organized religion', and spoke of 'the tragedy of Harry and Charlotte',[8] necessarily 'counterpointed' with the story of the convict in 'Old Man': 'All right. If that's the rule.' It is a kind of relinquishment of resistance that these characters are brought to; again Faulkner's reading of Hemingway comes into play. But in order to accept, the story must be placed within a history whose narrative coheres into 'all of it', a stasis of barely tolerable totality, the stereopticon and Keats's *Ode on a Grecian Urn* in 'The Bear', the continual urge to a single field of control.

2

Joseph Blotner's *William Faulkner's Library*, the *Paris Review* interview and *Faulkner at Nagano* all witness to the author's extraordinarily wide reading. This knowledge—and in many instances, his reading of major texts is annually or frequently repeated—is combined with his local historical and social experience, to construct an onward-going text of narrative skills, his *stories*—this is the constant term he uses in his interviews and responses to students. He also speaks, in the *Paris Review*, of Yoknapatawpha as another 'tool', together with his library: 'One of his tools the environment which he knows'. Within the tools of story and location he operates 'motion and motive'—that is, 'ambition, power, pleasure'. Morality is 'taken by force from the motion of which [man] is part. . .'. He always defines moral conscience, not as an imposed law, but rather as an instinctual given—not as a training inheritance, as it is, for example, in *Civilization and its Discontents*. It is 'the curse he had to accept from the Gods in order to gain from them the right to dream'; the right, that is, to invent stories which dramatize and probe 'motion and motive' and what 'the Gods' may infer. The dynastic designs in *The Sound and the Fury* (1929) and *Absalom, Absalom!* (1936) are located also in chronologies, a map and genealogies, to the point where, for instance, the last Sutpen disappears in 1910 and goes on living unknown in America. But such fictions, and those fictions called histories, interface as documents that constitute a culture:

> A culture exists in limited mobilities of complex fictions, which function as both permissive and restrictive patterns, stories and repeatable points of reference. These perform as a system only in so far as they constitute a mythology of behaviour and justification, a history of assumed origins and ends which can be used to permit both control and liberty—in government, sexuality and law. The arts, even in their most apparently non-representational twentieth-century forms, act as representations within this field.[9]

Faulkner's counterpointed stories resemble those of Fernand Braudel, who in the introduction to his *The Structures of Everyday Life* (1979), speaks of his model as layers written in 'the language . . . of the long term' in 'as wide a space as possible'. Hayden White in *Metahistory* (1973) speaks of a 'domain' in which 'theoretical concepts for "explaining" data' are replaced by 'a narrative structure for their presentation as an icon of events presumed to have occurred in times past'. Charles Olson, in *Maximus IV* (1962), writes of a possible poetics in which 'No event/is not penetrated, in intersection or collision with, an eternal/event.' White calls his method a poetics of history, and the epic writers Faulkner re-read—Balzac, Melville, Dostoevsky, Conrad, Shakespeare, and the scribes of the Old Testament[10]—find their poetics for what the epicist Ezra Pound called 'our address in time and space'. Hans Meyerhof introduces *The Philosophy of History in Our Time* (1959) as follows: 'Reason is often a poor guide to the deeply hidden, irrational strata from which many of the richest manifestations of human life draw their meaning and sustenance.' One reading of Faulkner's fictions is as artefacts of an historical consciousness shared with history and epic poetry, and as Warren I. Susman observes in *Culture as History* (1985), this creation of facts is never an easy task.

It is, however, essential if we are to sustain belief in that basis of creative change Faulkner calls hope. But his hope is played in a 'narrative game'[11] that requires a coherence of universals including justice, instinctual conscience and the ambiguities of law. These constitute the plot for narrative, his *story*. Recording orders. Fictions can be used to interrogate law, obedience, and that authenticity which masquerades as permissive innocence. Narrative is 'design' (*Paris Review* interview). Sutpen's Hundred is the paradigm of *story*. Sutpen's Grand Design ends in madness and anonymity; Faulkner's remains. Art rescues from truth. Faulkner does not cast an ideological sneer over the dynastic story, since he believes that 'Life is not interested in good and evil', and since 'people exist only in life, they must devote their time simply to being alive', even if being a human being itself means living 'compelled to make choices between good and evil sooner or later'. That is, the facts of 'moral conscience', which exists in an order that also contains, in the words of Quentin's father in *Absalom, Absalom!*, the values of 'courage and honour and pride and pity and love of justice and liberty'. Therefore, Faulkner, like his Quentin Compson, cannot hate his 'environment', and his characters often feel not guilt but outrage, bafflement and astonishment. Judgment on Sutpen's egotism, heartlessness and usages of his family and employees has to be open to the need for a pioneer's designer necessities. The Civil War is placed as a form of any conflict based on aggressive ideology—part of a curse, or in Rosa Coldfield's terms 'why God let us lose the War'. That landowners used their fellow human beings as instruments, both economic and sexual, is not a fact restricted to the South, nor in the nineteenth century nor in the West, *pace* Edward Said. For 'curse' read the human condition. As in 'A Justice', for The Man read 'du homme' or 'doom'. Who has not, like Ike McCaslin, in one way or another had to expiate for the father's actions? Justice and truth begin here, and law is the pattern of precedence of interference with these conditions. In one of his sixteen appearances in Faulkner, the Harvard and Heidelberg trained lawyer Gavin Stevens, county Attorney, admits:

> I am happy I was given the privilege of meddling with impunity in other people's affairs without really doing any harm by belonging to that avocation whose acolytes have been absolved in advance for holding justice above truth.

Which is exactly Faulkner's stated position. In *Intruder in the Dust* their basis is clear: 'it's all *now* you see.' But the 'environment' has now to be 'national' in a very peculiar distinction. In Chapter 7, Stevens comes out with the politics of justification:

> Only a few of us know that only from homogeneity comes anything of a people or for a people of durable and lasting value—the literature, the art, the science, that minimum of government and police which is the meaning of freedom and liberty, and perhaps most valuable of all a national character worth anything in a crisis.

So 'the North' has to be resisted because 'national' here means 'the privilege of setting [the Negro] free ourselves', since nobody else in America can. In Chapter 9, Stevens recognizes what Faulkner reiterates in interviews and responses: 'the injustice is ours, the South's. We must expiate and abolish it ourselves.' And this is further embedded in what Stevens abjures his nephew Chick Mallison to enact as instinctual conscience: 'Something you must always be unable to bear. . . . Injustice and outrage and dishonour and shame.' In Chapter 10, the choice is paralleled with 'the position of a German after 1933 who had no other alternative between being either a Nazi or a Jew, or the present Russian (European too for that matter) who hasn't even that but must

Law, Justice and Justification in William Faulkner

either be a communist or dead. . . .'.

Chick Mallison moves to rescue Lucas Beauchamp from the rough justice of lynch-law out of this complex basis of conscience, a sense of justice prior to local law and racist fact. But the break with Jefferson majority is as difficult as it is for Huckleberry Finn breaking with his 'environment', and like him Chick has to find resources against his immediate education, just as McCaslin has to (Huck's 'environment' was governed by the Fugitive Slave law). He can, however, revert to the prior order of Miss Habersham (Chapter 4): 'He's a Negro and your uncle's a man . . . Lucas knew it would take a child—or an old woman like me: someone not concerned with probability, with evidence.' But she and Chick need the practical skills and perceptions of Alick Sanders (Chapter 9). In the event, sheriff law is curtailed (Chapter 7) by Gowrie pistol law, to prevent two Negroes digging up a white grave! Gun law is never justice, always rough justice or 'how the West was won'. But it is the cool sheriff who puts Chick's discovery into law, not lawyer Stevens, and certainly not the Gowrie clan, or the People or the mob, with its urge to lynching and vigilantism. It is the sheriff—'silver shield on his breast . . . real pistol in his pocket'—who identifies the murderer's gun: 'A German Luger automatic. . . . Like the one Buddy McCallum brought home from France in 1919 and traded that summer for a pair of fox hounds' (Chapter 8). But the Gowries and the Snopeses, according to Rosa Coldfield, have their roots in the Sutpens. When Lee surrendered to Grant in 1865 the South 'would realize that it was now paying for having erected its economic edifice not on the rock of stern morality but on the shifting sands of opportunism and moral brigandage'. As early as *Sartoris* in 1929 Faulkner partly dehistoricized these figures into 'pawns' for 'the Player, and the game he plays'. The Player pre-exists law and persists even in the most ambivalent evaluation:

> Perhaps Sartoris is the game itself—a game outmoded and played with pawns shaped too late and to an old dead pattern, and of which the Player himself is a little wearied. For there is death in the Sound of it and a glamorous fatality, like silver pennons down rushing at sunset, or a dying fall of horns along the road to Roncevaux.

Such Tennysonian cadences for 'flags in the dust', barely spiced up with the term 'glamorous' taken from the American romanticisms of Booth Tarkington and early Fitzgerald, were among Twain's targets in *Life on the Mississippi* in 1883. The dynasts, the knitting machine or the Great Will need gingering up by 1929. It is not, as some critics believe, so much an ambivalence for aristocrats as fascination with doomed sacrificial people, those he celebrates in *Pylon* (1935, four years before *The Wild Palms*). The reckless air circus performers appear as descendants of Bayard Sartoris and his doomed flier brother, but now locationless within their own laws of risk and sacrifice: 'No ties: no place where you were born and have to go back to it now and then if it's only to hate the damn place good and comfortable for a day or two.'

McCaslin's doom is inherited from the ledgers of land transactions and their revealed lusts for conquests, wills, dynastic securities. 'I can't repudiate it', he says, because he is fixed in the ambivalently legal line of sale from Ikkemotubbe to himself, which betrayed another law, a trust from God: 'to hold the earth mutual and intact in the communal anonymity of brotherhood'. At Nagano, Faulkner said that twenty-five years ago—that would be 1930—'In theory, I thought communism would be very good for people . . . this [today] is not the communism that I thought I understood.' Like many other Americans in the 1930s, Faulkner found no state of law, justice and society to which he might give his allegiance. But his allegiance would in any case not be based on ideology[12] since the Player rules. Men and women of trained analytical intelligence and a wide range of learning are missing, and so is the reciprocity of love, and women who are actively intelligent and in their own way. Magnificent storytelling, his 'polyphonic rhetoric',[13] directs energies towards grotesques, in Sherwood Anderson's sense—a main form of American fiction through to the present day. And who can deny that American politics and economic power, as in any other nation, is controlled by grotesques? The Great Will fosters grotesques, weirdly representative outlaws from mutual aid and co-operation. Faulkner needed fables of directed force within the Player's realm, and challenges to that universality which proved human capacities for endurance and resistance, law-breakers of Circumstance.

A Fable (1954) documents the victory and death of an army corporal who leads a mutiny for unofficial armistice during the 1918 fighting in World War I. Part of the universality is provided from parallels with Christ's sacrificial passion. An historical legend is made exemplary: the mutual agreement of French, German, British and American soldiers to disobey military law. A German general flies over to discuss with the Allies' generals how to continue the war conducted and continued by themselves, politicians and profiteers. Their war is now against a universal of mutuality: brotherhood, mutiny, a cease-fire. The focus is an embodiment of Faulkner's concept of instinctual knowledge-conscience, the Corporal, with twelve disciples of various nationalities on both sides of a No Man's Land of peace and good will on earth towards men. He is also one of Faulkner's disobedient sons, a breaker of patriarchal law, the illegitimate son of the supreme French commander, and born in a stable. The parody is reinforced: this is Passion Week and the Corporal will be executed with thieves.

As Henry Sutpen repudiates Colonel Sutpen, and relinquishes his estate, and Ike McCaslin repudiates his father and his estate, to expose sinister authority, so does the Corporal. By extension Faulkner himself repudiates that authoritarian paternalism embodied in the Christian myth, a humiliation to the human, for whom the son must sacrifice himself for ideals of truth and justice beyond Father law. Chick Mallison disobeys the law. Joe Christmas is sacrificed to the Player, the Dark Diceman or Circumstance, whose agent is Percy Grimm. The Corporal's grave is exploded and found empty, but the absent body becomes not a resurrected god but the human example, the Unknown Soldier—the son of sons killed in all paternalistic wars. Faulkner's criticism of Christianity exemplifies an element of the Nobel prize speech in 1950: that man 'is immortal, not because he alone among creatures has an inexhaustible voice, but because he has a soul, a spirit capable of compassion and sacrifice and endurance'. The large rhetorical outpouring of the prose is part of the story's plot of overwhelming conviction. The central issue is certainly clear, and can be condensed from the Marshal's speeches. No human being can confer freedom on his fellows—which is also part of Faulkner's case in the American Negro issue. At one point the Marshal concludes in the classic position of Satan in *Paradise Regained*:

> I don't bribe you with money. I give you liberty. . . . Why else have I offered to buy my—our—security with things which most men not only do not want but on the contrary do well to fear and flee from, like liberty and freedom? Oh yes, I can destroy you tomorrow morning and save us—for a time. And if I must, I will. Because I believe in man within his capacities and limitations . . . he must endure, at least until he himself invents evolves produces a better tool that he to substitute for himself.

He offers his son that 'power, matchless and immeasurable' he has himself inherited and his son has already shown himself capable of using:

> You will be God; holding [mankind] forever through a far, far stronger ingredient than his simple lusts and appetites: by his triumphant and ineradicable folly, his deathless passion for being led, mystified, and deceived. . . .

In that 'infinite capacity—no: passion—for unfact' in which 'there is no content actually' lies man's stupidity: 'So once more: take the earth.' Then the Marshal gives another aspect of Faulkner's limited human justice under the Player's law:

> that in him which will enable him to outlast even his wars . . . to outlast even his enslavement to the demonic progeny of his own mechanical curiosity, from which he will emancipate himself by that once ancient tried-and-true method by which slaves have always freed themselves: by incalcating their masters with the slaves' own vices—in this case the vice of war and that other vice which is no vice at all but is the . . . warrant of man's immortality: his deathless folly.

While the Marshal temporarily takes the rôle of the Angel showing Adam man's future, he includes man's populating a new star, 'after the earth cools'—'still talking, still planning . . . more efficient and louder than before, yet it too inherent with the same old primordial fault'. The son's revolt is weak because it repudiates that need for conflict and disaster on which Faulkner insisted, for instance, at Nagano. But there is no question of absolute divine control (the Marshal himself inherits his rule) or pure human democracy or what Eric Bentley called 'heroic vitalism'.[14] This is a fable of the circumstances. Uniquely in Faulkner, a further challenge, and a cause of the father's act of destruction, is the Corporal's power to inspire love. Faulkner knows that the idea of a god-inspiring love is absurd, or at the most neurotic. The only too familiar modern cry of 'all you need is love' is there in the Corporal's message: 'all we ever need to do was just to say, Enough of this.' But Faulkner has no justice with love inside it. The inefficiency of love cannot prevent conflict of authorities, nor can it eliminate that desire which links Bayard Sartoris and his brother to the airmen in *Pylon* and now the young R.A.F. officer here—the thirst for glory. Faulkner's suspicion is firm, and it includes a suspicion of causes of the Civil War:

> The laurel of glory, provided it was even moderately leafed, had human blood on it; that was permissable only when the motherland itself was at stake. Peace abolished it, and that man who would choose between glory and peace had best let his voice be small indeed.

The R.A.F. enthusiast's uniform is eroded by phosphorous from dummy bullets substituted by the Corporal's peace disciples. He commits suicide rather than exist without glory.

The Snopes characteristic evil by commerce and money— the key evil in Hemingway's *A Farewell to Arms* and *For Whom the Bell Tolls* (1940), in Cummings's *The Enormous Room* (1922) and elsewhere, Dos Passos' *The Grand Design* (1949) and Pound's *Cantos*—is particularly engendered by those who manufacture war as their tool, an evil 'grand design' far beyond the folly of Thomas Sutpen, or even Flem Snopes. This is the higher law of corruption:

> a council where trained military experts, dedicated as irrevocably to war as nuns are married to God . . . the Prime Ministers, and Premiers and Secretaries, the cabinet ministers and senators and chancellors . . . the board chairmen of the vast establishments which produce the munitions and shoes and tinned foods . . . the priests of simple money . . . the politicians, the lobbyists, the owners and publishers of newspapers and the ordained ministers of churches, and all the other accredited travelling representatives of the vast

solvent organizations and fraternities and movements, which control, [by] coercion and cajolery man's morals and actions and all his mass-values for affirmation or negation—all that vast powerful terror-inspiring representation which, running all democracy's affairs in peace, comes indeed into its own in war, finding its true apotheosis then . . . a design vast in its intention to demolish a frontier, and vaster still in its furious intent to obliterate a people. . . .

Since this design is so historically perpetual, it might just as well be called Fate or the Player or Circumstance. Peace and war are not separate. Reasons of state are always military. The individual is organized towards the ends of organization, that logistical society which continually gives birth to itself. The crucial event in *A Fable* is therefore the Marshal's statement to his old friend the Quartermaster General—that is, the master of state logistics and their evil laws:

> We and it . . . and our whole unregenerate and unregeneratable kind . . . our tight close jealous unchallengeable hierarchy . . . we have had to make this last desperate cast in order to hold our last desperate and precarious place in it.

His ally in the dice-throw is a Judas, therefore, 'one of his close and familiar own—as always', but part of the logistical design. He offers the Corporal sacrificial martyrdom and escape back to the Father. The son can only reply: 'There's nothing to be afraid of. Nothing's worth it.' He is one of Faulkner's primal figures; he cannot read, and his only and pivotal belief is that human beings are not worthless.

The priest-confessor sent to him represents the church's fear of Christ figures—as classically in *The Brothers Karamazov*; he believes it was 'pagan and bloody' Rome that made Christ a martyr, not Christ's sacrifice. But he kneels before the Corporal, begging to be saved, and then commits suicide with a sentry's bayonet which he somewhat blasphemously identifies with the spear that pierced Christ on the Cross. One British officer attempts to identify with unranked commoners by giving up his commission. Disgracing his regiment by copulating with a girl in public permits him to resign and become an ordinary soldier, a runner. Gathering information about the peace mutiny, he gains respect for the Corporal and his disciples: 'His prototype had only man's

Law, Justice and Justification in William Faulkner

natural propensity for evil to contend with; this one faces all the scarlet-and-brazen impregnability of general staffs.' He attempts to follow the Corporal's example, and justify his own existence—he is a St. Paul figure—with a second mutiny, but he is shot down in No Man's Land, his 'voice crying out of the soundless rush of flame which enveloped half of his body neatly from heel through navel through chin: "They can't kill us! They can't! Not dare not: they can't!" ' The revolts are as suicidal as they are necessary. At the Marshal's Arc de Triomphe funeral procession, the runner bursts from the crowd:

> not a man but a mobile and upright scar, on crutches, he had one arm and one leg, one entire side of his hatless head was one hairless eyeless scar, he wore a filthy dinner jacket from the left breast of which depended on their barber-pole ribbon, a British Military Cross and Distinguished Conduct Medal, and a French *Medaille Militaire*.

This grotesque of sacrificial justification flings the latter at the cortège in contempt, and, like Lee Goodwin, is manhandled by the mob into the gutter. As the Quartermaster lifts his head and shoulders up, he ends the book with a last statement of desperate dignity, and its response:

> 'That's right. . . . Tremble. I'm not going to die. Never.'
> 'I am not laughing', the old man bending over him said.
> 'What you see are tears.'

Thirty-five years later, 'man's deathless folly' has not changed, of course, but perhaps equanimity and compassion before it is too stoic. Certainly, the Marshal figure remains in control— god and devil, omniscient tempter who appears to uphold man but contemptuously sacrifices him to Design, the avatar of the Leader as agent of the Player.

But the story of *A Fable* does not tidily resolve, even if Faulkner does need to rest back into permanent Circumstance and its Law, a stasis of fiction and truth that both condemns and transcends. Hemingway's 'separate peace' for Nick Adams in 1925 has at least become a mutiny, and Faulkner senses, as the Beat generation writers did in the late 1950s, that mutineers can be heroes for our time, that the rebels are the heroes, not the conformists, bureaucrats and the power hierarchy. But he does not give single allegiance to either his Judas with 'a knowing, almost handsome metropolitan face', or the Corporal or the Marshal. *A Fable* is a compendium on the significances of justified strife and its concommitant futility. The Corporal's 'Don't be afraid' is at least something beyond 'The horror! The horror!' But Conrad is still near to Faulkner with Marlow's sense of 'the outraged law, like the bursting shells', 'your own capacity for faithlessness', and 'inborn strength. Principles won't do . . . you want a deliberate belief.' Conrad never expected justice, nor does Faulkner. Sceptical faith is a strategy for cohering a story from an inside narrative of compulsion. It still has to be a barricade against the cynical praise of Sgt. Hartman in *Full Metal Jacket* for John Whitman, who massacred twelve Texans in Austin, and Lee Harvey Oswald, because 'God had a hard-on for marines because we kill everything we see, we keep heaven packed with fresh souls.'

3

Thomas Sutpen encounters justice as his dynastic design crumbles under challenge. Continuity must find the law of its desires: legitimacy through legitimate white male heirs, the point of breaking the law or taboo or marriage—he suggests to Rosa Coldfield that 'they try it first and if it was a boy and lived, they would be married'. That story has to end with Rosa's coercion of Quentin Compson to see who the remnants are at Sutpen's Hundred, the container of law and lawlessness, a house of frontier barbarism and necessary American settlement, façades of gentility and entry into legal society, his 'fixed goal' against 'eventuality', 'circumstance against human nature, his own fallible judgment and mortal clay against not only human but natural forces'. The Sutpen boy accepted Tidewater law, and discovered that law extended to Haiti, miscegenation and his first son Charles Bon, and his legal purchase of land from Ikkemotubbe, which illegally contradicts another law: land is not for buying and selling. In any case, Ikkemotubbe is a usurper ('The Old People' and 'A Justice') as well as an illegal seller of tribal land. Sutpen, like the Chickasaw, inherits slaves—a further kind of legalized

Law, Justice and Justification in William Faulkner

illegality. Even his transference of French classicism to the style for a dynastic house is a sign of false authority through 'baronial splendour'. Becoming friends at the University of Mississippi, Henry introduces Charles Bon to his sister Judith, preparing the route through miscegenation, to incest, and to Bon's statement to Henry: 'So it's miscegenation, not incest, you can't bear.'

The Sutpen epic of dynastic endurance is in these ways laid down in an enclosure of judgments and freedoms. Thomas's outraged questioning of his failure is from a man unable to bring knowledge to bear against universal inevitables. Beyond that and into the enclosing narrative, Shreve McCannon's Canadian outsider scepticism and Quentin's admission of baffled inheritance frame unchangeable motions of stasis. Rosa Coldfield can only see Sutpen's demonic energy, a blasphemous Prometheus in the wilderness, 'fiend, blackguard and devil', 'ogre or djinn', a lawless man within in his own conception of order. Her own lawful existence reduces her to a 'crucified child' confronting Sutpen's bronzed Negro-brown face in the white western church image of Christian darkness, compounded of night, Hell, dark skins and the traffic of slavery. Quentin is compelled into the impotence of a story-ridden South, 'peopled with garrulous outraged baffled ghosts'. Civil war and the Sutpen father and children—broken laws and orders, under the novel's Old Testament title—coincide in a story of double secession, knowledge withheld and then made visible by narrative revelations to 1936 readers over seventy years later. Faulkner even confers legal studies on Bon and Henry in Chapter 4:

> Bon was reading law. He would be, would almost have to, since only that could have made his residence bearable regardless of what reason he may have brought with him for remaining—this, the perfect setting for his dilatory indolence: this digging into musty Blackstone and Coke where, of an undergraduate body still numbered in two figures, the law school probably (consisted of six others besides Henry and himself—yes, he corrupted Henry to the law; Henry changed in midterm.

So they inherit European common law as a dead apparatus in the territory of Sutpen and Ikkemotubbe, and Secession.

No law intervenes between the dead compendium and Mississippi 'fatality'. Quentin's father puts it to his son: Sutpen 'had been too successful, you see: his was that solitude of contempt and distrust which success brings to him who gained it because he was strong instead of merely lucky.' This evasion falsifies out of limited understanding. In Faulkner's story, after the 'holocaust' (Chapter 1) caused by Secession, the Sutpens move, like the South, into their 'destiny' (Chapter 3). Faulkner's paragraph recalls the stasis of Coleridge's 'Kubla Khan'—the Hundred in a former lake 'welling from quiet springs' and the family

> [floated] in sunny suspension, felt the first subterranean movement toward the outlet, the gorge which would be the land's catastrophe . . . feeling the dark set . . . not even aware that that point was approaching.

The Civil War is the centre of the story, for family and nation. For Henry it signals, as it will in *A Fable*, fathers' betrayals of sons. Temple Drake's sense of God denying the required knowledge is prefigured in Henry's reply to his father's command that Judith may not marry Bon, and so is the Corporal's reply to his Judas, and Wilbourne's self-interrogation:

> now it won't be much longer now and then we won't have anything left: honour nor pride nor God since God quit us four years ago only He never thought it necessary to tell us . . . nothing matters except that there is the old mindless meat that don't even care if it was defeat or victory, that won't even die.

Henry will have to confront Charles Bon, who saved his life, towards the end of the War, and shoot him—but only after Bon has said: 'I'm the nigger that's going to sleep with your sister. Unless you stop me, Henry.' Wash kills the seducer of his 15-year-old daughter, and is himself shot down by a posse—illegally, that is. The coherent mess of lives in Chapters 6 to 9 concludes Faulkner's family romance'. On a frozen night in the North, Quentin tells of the frozen night in the South when he discovers Henry in bed in the Hundred, 'the Domain', with a 'reek in slow protracted violence with a smell of desolation and decay as if the wood of which it were built were flesh'. Democratic speeds have slowed to stasis behind a door that can only be broken down, not opened. In Quentin it produces a stasis of anguish: 'Nevermore of peace. Nevermore of piece. Nevermore Nevermore Nevermore.' The echo of Poe's croaks is apt, since Quentin is a prisoner of the narrative, as Henry is imprisoned in his legal house since he can be arrested for murder. The dynasty ends in Clytemnestra, daughter of Thomas and a Negro slave, setting fire to the house, Henry and herself, to subvert law, and an idiot descendant howling in its ashes: 'But they couldn't catch him. . .'.

Laws of various kinds catch all the main characters—'the old ineradicable rhythm'. Sutpen lived in titan conflict, an American version of the Hesiodic myth of resistance to Legal Authority as Zeus. In *The Life of the Mind in America*, Perry Miller writes that within the American nineteenth century lies a long debate on the nature of law and the individual, law repeatedly meaning the father God's universal law, with explanatory examples from botany, biology, geology and physics, according to taste and temperament. Appeals to determinist constants or universalism are confused to the point where some legal theorists praise the confusion as sublime and 'as chaotic as human nature'.[15] Better that than codificatory legalists trying to grasp the divine. The situation is Faulkner's. Shreve McCannon translates Sutpen as 'this Faustus, this demon, this Beelzebub' (Chapter 6) fleeing from 'his Creditor's outraged face', from the 'bailiff hand' waiting to claim him, so that his soul can be legally claimed. Quentin counters with Sutpen's 'innocence' (Chapter 7). That is, like Faulkner's idiots and primitives he is under compulsion, therefore an outlaw and therefore in a particular sense imposed upon by his condition into permissive innocence:

> All of a sudden he discovered, not what he wanted to do but what he just had to do, had to do it whether he wanted to or not, because if he did not do it he knew that he could never live with himself for the rest of his life, never live with what all the men and women that had died to make him had left inside of him to pass on. . . . And that at the very moment when he discovered what it was, he found that this was the last thing in the world he was equipped to do. . . .

So a knowledge challenges universal order which contains a law of failure—hubris against the Dark Diceman. Parenthetic clauses build lengthy sentences of inclusive persuasion to dramatize inevitability, a totality of 'all of it', history as space of time in which to justify and judge behaviour and its limited choices.

But the Overreacher is innocent by universal law. The Creditor will claim his victim within his programme. The narrative believer is left holding the frayed end of sterility and impotence, the results of 'luck' and 'innocence'. Quentin inherits precisely the boy Sutpen's knowledge: 'he knew that to do what he had to do in order to live with himself he would have to think it out as straight as a man would.' Innocence in knowledge is part of existential law, part of the claims of God the Father Creditor. No excuse to discover too late (Chapter 7) your 'impediment was innocence' and that part of it was marrying Eulalia Bon 'in good faith'. Steve McCannon voices a central ambivalence: that being inside the theatre of permissive innocence might be a pleasure: 'the South is fine isn't it. . . . It's better than Ben Hur, isn't it' (Chapter 7). The show must go on.

One structuring factor of *Go Down, Moses* (1942)—Moses the Old Testament bringer of stonily engraven tablet of God's law—is the descent of Lucius Quintus Carothers McCaslin from two centuries of dynastic series, a fetishist programme masked in an enclosure of violent mobilities that parody change. The beginning is again land acquisition from the Indian; and also acquisition, from the Indian, a quadroon slave and her son, Sam Fathers, Ikkemotubbe's unacknowledged son. At one point economic atonement for sexual and parental crime—miscegenation and incest once again, among other acts—takes the form of Lucius's legacy for Turl, his son by Tomasina, his own daughter. The ledgers Ike McCaslin, his grandson discovers, record a legacy of money and sex as a wasted energy in an entropic society. One large passage in 'The Bear' carries a story of money, sexuality, slavery and perverse loneliness fused into farrago of impotence, a paradigm of illegitimate powers which will lead to a proud finale in Lucas Beauchamp, Lucius McCaslin's part-Negro grandson, the centre of law and lynch-law in *Intruder in the Dust*.

Law, Justice and Justification in William Faulkner

He refuses to play 'nigger' in racist social law, and uses his position as a strategic stereotype with which to establish his integrity under law. In 'Delta Autumn' Ike McCaslin paraphrases the Genesis story of creation: man is the 'overseer' of the earth with a clear contract—that is, his legality in a world he did not create and is not a commercial proposition: 'to hold the earth mutual and intact in the communal anonymity of brotherhood'. Holding to this contract, he has to live for decades in an isolation from property, family and social position. In 'The Fire and the Hearth', Lucas obtains his McCaslin legacy on his twenty-first birthday, and moves into his own house on the family property, legally. But 'one of McCaslin's Negroes', Rider, kills a white man using a loaded dice in a crap game and is hunted down and lynched while the sheriff's deputy, an impotent racist, refuses to intervene, since he needs the townspeople's votes.[16] 'If it isn't going to be law', the lynchers are in power, the lawless centre of violation, part of primitivist law and taboo which undermines the state.

Ike's stasis of loneliness in fact begins out of primitivist initiations from Sam Fathers—manhood rituals of beast killing, the hunt and the blooding—an inheritance of fixed tribal lore and law, transferred to a white boy in 1879. Faulkner's long sentence is an onward-going motion of connection that establishes the mystical transmission: '. . . they were the white boy, marked forever, and the old dark man sired on both sides by savage kings, who had marked him, whose bloody hands had merely formally consecrated him. . . .' In fact, the totemism for them is enacted as preservation of the bear, while the official white man's hunt is for a killing: in the words of Claude Lévi-Strauss, 'not because it is "good to eat" but because it is "good to think" '.[17] Through this transmission from the pre-white, pre-urban and subversive law, Ike has to live in permanent stasis within adopted ancestors, 'the old people': 'it was he, the boy, who was the guest here and Sam Fathers's voice the mouthpiece of the host.' But over all is 'the eye of the ancient immortal Umpire', and the scene is his: 'they stood motionless, breathing deep and quiet and steady', in 'unchanging light'. For Sam Fathers, the buck not killed is an avatar of the Umpire: 'Chief . . . Grandfather'.

In the final section of *Go Down, Moses*, Lucas Beachamp's old wife Molly asks Gavin Stevens to find her grandson, Samuel. Unknown to her, he is about to be executed for murder in Chicago—a man who took Ike's advice to Roth's young woman: 'Go back North. Marry: a man of your own race. That's the only salvation for you . . . Marry a black man'.

But John Brown is also part of the Creditor's design—that part which included the provision of free will, interpreted here, as so often in such myths, as law-breaking and outlawry. Faulkner's words for Him will later be used for the Marshal in 1954:

> He didn't hope He just waited because He had made them. . . . He must admit them or else admit His equal somewhere and so be no longer God and therefore accept responsibility for what He Himself had done in order to live with Himself in His lonely and paramount heaven.

God eventually is under the same law as Thomas Sutpen, Quentin Compson and John Brown. Ike McCaslin's relinquishment is part of 'the primal Absolute which contained all', including 'an Isaac born into a later life than Abraham's and repudiating immolation: fatherless. . .'. The Umpire watches profit-making rich slavers and 'the descendants of rich slavers', 'the medicine-shows of pulpiteers' in politics and religion, and the whole show of exploitive industrial manufacturers. Then one single man says, as Melville believed Hawthorne had said, 'No, in thunder', breaking the law:

> one simple enough to believe that horror and outrage were first and simply horror and outrage and was crude enough to act upon that . . . who did not bother Him with cajolery and abjuration then pleading then threat and not even bothered to inform Him in advance. . . . He said *My name is Brown* too and the other *So is mine*. . . .

In reply to His queries about 'your Associates, your Committee, your Officers . . . your Parliamentary Procedures', Brown states his singular opposition: 'I am just against the weak because they are niggers being held in bondage by the strong just because they are white.' And he says this with his 'long ancestral musket' in hand. The Creditor comments:

Law, Justice and Justification in William Faulkner

'Apparently they can learn nothing save through suffering, remember nothing save when underlined in blood.' Nothing in Faulkner's *Essays, Speeches and Public Letters* has further comment, but it is clear that Nancy Mannigoe will be an additional 'simple' opposer, ten years later. Unheard within John Brown's justification is Ike McCaslin's:

> I could say I don't know why I must do it but that I do know I have got to because I have got myself to have to live with for the rest of my life and all I want is peace to do it in.

The control once again comes from instinctual moral conscience as activating knowledge. But Keats's *Ode* is again present, and with other Keats statements:

> It covers all things that touch the heart.... Courage and honour and pride, and pity and love of justice and of liberty. They all touch the heart, and the heart holds to become truth, as far as we know truth.

The terms of heart law against head law penetrated American discussion of law since the founding of the nation and remain unresolved. Faulkner's technological image is accurate. The stereopticon, in the words of the *Oxford English Dictionary*, is 'a double magic lantern arranged to combine two images of the same object or scene upon a screen, so as to produce the appearance of solidity as in a stereoscope'. The immediate context combines the Keats *Ode* with the land curse, the two McCaslins juxtaposed and alien now to each other against their ravaged patrimony, the dark and ravaged fatherland still prone and panting from its etherless operation—that is, the Civil War. As one McCaslin raises his hand in the small room, he transforms it into an enclosure of 'all', and Faulkner's huge sentence is its violent stasis: 'as the stereopticon condenses into one instantaneous field the myriad minutiae of its scope'. Against its tightness, Ike has only 'I am free ... Sam Fathers set me free.' This is what Faulkner called his 'pageant rite'.[18]

'The Bear' exemplifies Faulkner's memory theatre, in Frances Yates's sense of a memorial container of history,[19] and his prose ideally interlocks parentheses and clauses into a rhetorical strategy of legitimation: 'one sentence, between one cap and one period ... if possible, on one pinhead . . . not only the present but the whole past on which it depends and which keeps overtaking the present, second by second'.[20] No future, since a maze or a pinhead have no future, and memory is a spatial, non-chronological accumulation. But the Work includes the dilemma of Law: that there is, or might be, a wisdom to be discovered 'beyond even that learned through suffering necessary for a man to distinguish between liberty and license'. As Empson observed of Milton's epic obsession to 'justify the ways of God to man':

> That his feelings were crying out against his appalling theology in favour of freedom, happiness and the pursuit of truth was I think not obvious to him, and it is this part of the dramatic complex which is thrust upon us by the repeated all.[21]

Faulkner was, in fact, seriously conscious of this disjuncture. But the intelligent outlaw whose knowledge probes the present, in order to bring about the future in a changed condition, still cannot appear—what Robert Duncan once called 'the outlaw who has the strength of his own lawfulness'. John Brown is defeated, and the characters and opinion that emerge from *Essays, Speeches and Public Letters* participate in the conditions of that defeat. Tensions between law and lawlessness, natural law and institutionalized law, stasis and change, urban industrialization and what T. S. Eliot—a firm supporter of *I'll Take my Stand*—called 'the life of significant soil', hunter's rights and victim's rights, and the liberty of property and the liberty of community and mutual aid—these are the vectors of American legal conduct from the first: from Williams Bradford's Plymouth community renouncing mutual aid in 1622, through the ninth and twelfth of Crèvecoeur's *Letters from an American Farmer* in 1782, to Henry Adams deciding in 1904 that 'good was order, law, unity—evil was disorder, anarchy, multiplicity', but what then is truth? Are law and order accidental? All that Faulkner can do for continuity is to reiterate in 1956: 'the thesis which I'm always hammering at: that man is indestructible because of his simple will to freedom'.[22]

Law, Justice and Justification in William Faulkner

But *Sanctuary* and the Snopes trilogy dramatize the success of freedom and indestructibility as truths outside communal law and order. Faulkner needed *As I Lay Dying* (1930) as a non-criminal plot exemplifying his 'simple' axiom: 'I simply imagined a group of people and subjected them to the simple universal natural catastrophes, which are flood and fire, with a simple natural motive to give direction to their progress.' Only Darl Bundren becomes an outlaw, detained as a criminal lunatic by the state, with little resistance from his family whose coherence is neither law nor love but clan reciprocity for endurance, a peasant reinforcement. Its radial centre is Jewel, illegitimate son of his mother's passionate adultery with a parson, and instance of legitimate natural vitality, who comes to challenge the Creditor or Jehovah: 'If there is a God what the Hell is He for?' It is Jewel who sacrifices what he loves most, his horse, to his mother's death—in Jung's terms: 'the libido directed towards the mother actually symbolized by her as a horse'.[23] Cash makes the mother's coffin as a transference of nature through laws of human technology—not so much love as an offering of skills. In fact, the mother repudiated love as just a word, 'just a shape to fill a lack. . . . My aloneness had been violated and then made whole: time, Anse, love, what you will, outside the circle.' She joins Faulkner's general refusal of Christianity and of easy-going definitions of love:

> sin, love and fear are just sounds that people who have never sinned nor loved nor feared have for what they never had until they forget the words . . . [sin] is the instrument ordained by God who created sin, to sanctify that sin He had created . . . garments which would remove in order to shape and coerce the terrible blood to the forlorn echo of the dead word high in the air.

God's law and logos are imposed, and broken by a prior wordless law. As Faulkner told his 1956 interviewer: this story 'took command of the dream'—and to the necessity of the plot he gave the Conradian term 'implacable', a word for the laws the Bundren family fulfil.

Like Sutpen, then, Addie has the necessity of her own design, even if she does believe that Darl 'was touched by God himself and considered queer by us mortals'—the tradition, that is, of divine madness as a cause and therefore a legitimation. Cash defines madness within a concept of 'balance', a law of equilibrium a joiner and carpenter would know, a 'universal' and 'natural' stasis: 'ain't none of us pure crazy and ain't none of us pure sane until the balance of us talks him that-a-way.' And he adds, after seeing the courthouse next to the monument to the Confederate dead—emblems of another disequilibrium and secession—'it's better to build a tight chicken-coop than shoddy court-house.' Once the mother is interred, Anse can release the comedy—'God's will be done. . . . Now I can get them teeth'—and the legitimizing myth of Job: 'I am chosen of the Lord, for who He loveth, so doeth He chastitheth. But I be done if He don't take some curious ways to show it, seems like.' Darl's eight affirmatory cries of 'yes', in his cell, parallel Quentin Compson's 'I don't hate it' and the British officer in *A Fable*—'they can't kill us!' They affirm endurance within universal balance, just as the six white fanatics do as they constitute the carrier of plot for *Light in August* (1932)

4

They include a rigid Calvinist wallowing in legalistic paternalist Christianity: a former Presbyterian minister, neurotic after training in God-enforcement; a liberal fanatic for Negro rights, descendant of New England abolitionists or law-breakers against the Fugitive Slave Law; a man motivated out of puritanical guilt, and God-controlled debt; and a young inheritor of the extra-legal habit of vigilantism and the whole rigmarole of special pleading that the religious state enforces. Percy Grimm is also under direct control from the Player as he moves human figures on his Board. At the moment of murder and castration of Joe Christmas, Grimm therefore transcends individualism and becomes an agent, legally self-permitting, and static within the game (Chapter 19):

> He stopped, motionless in mid stride. Above the blunt, cold rake of his automatic his face had that serene luminousness of angels in church windows. He was moving again almost before he had stopped, with that lean, swift, blind obedience

Law, Justice and Justification in William Faulkner

to whatever Player moved him on the Board. . . . He seemed indefatiguable, not flesh and blood, as if the Player who moved him for pawn likewise found him breath.

Angel permission includes whatever this 25-year-old National Guard captain, who lives to generate manhood lost in missing the War, needs for pure definition, to reach permissive innocence, to kill within authority and, therefore, law. Faulkner gives this as Grimm's fate, and the prose fuses social, psychological and historical into an exemplary behaviour, a design, which engenders assassination—that legality from agency with which the United States is only too familiar in its history of vigilantism and rough justice. His life is 'opening before him, uncomplex and inescapable as a barren corridor, completely freed now of ever again having to think or decide'. His uniform, his racism, his belief that 'the American is superior to all other races and that American uniform is superior to all men, and that all that would ever be required of him in payment for his belief, this privilege, would be his own life, and his commander's directive—'We got to preserve order. . . . We must let the law take its course. The law, the nation.' This is the classic design of justificatory justice. Its extension is the military and the state's programme in *A Fable*. As the commander says: 'It is the right of no civilian to sentence a man to death. And we, the soldiers in Jefferson, are the ones to see to that.' As for the victims: 'there won't be any need for them even to talk.'

The lawyer Stevens believes that Joe Christmas's grandmother wanted him to 'die "decent", as she put it. Decently hung by a Force, a principle; not burned or hacked or dragged by a Thing'. The religious maniac Hines, 'mad as a hatter and completely hoarse, preaching lynching, telling people how he had grandfathered the devil's spawn and had kept it in trust for this day', is the agent of Christian assault on black people—including Indians, called the Black Man by the Puritans, and witches, equally agents of the Enemy. The horror is clear in this scene of agency, permission and Christianity, and the definitions have entered Christmas himself, imaged by Faulkner as conflict between white and black blood in him. At Nagano Faulkner repudiated blood lore and its law,[24] but these are the terms of agency and the nation's beliefs. At

West Point in 1962, his last public appearance, Faulkner described Christmas as 'one of the most tragic figures I can think of because he himself didn't know who he was—... would never know'. To a Japanese student in 1955: 'man's immortality is that he is faced with a tragedy which he can't beat and he still tries to do something about it.'[25] Tragedy is therefore the effect of law and justice, of the Player, injustice in its racist form in Circumstance. Lawyer Stevens even goes so far as to say that the racial situation is 'not basically a moral problem'. At the University of Virginia, Faulkner said that Gavin Stevens's surmise that a 'conflict of blood' is 'an assumption, a rationalization which Stevens made. That is, the people that destroyed [Joe Christmas] made rationalizations about what he was. They decided what he was'. Then he uses the language he employed for Sutpen, Quentin Compson and Ike McCaslin and others, a variant of his existential endurance formula: 'his only salvation in order to live with himself was to repudiate mankind, to live outside the human race. And he tried to do that but nobody would let him.'

For Christmas to be 'tragic' he had to run within the control of Mississippi August light as Grecian light, 'Olympian in it somewhere', 'a luminosity older than our Christian civilization', the stasis of injustice. In 1956, Faulkner wrote: 'I must go on record as opposing the forces outside the South which would use legal or police compulsion to eradicate that evil (the race problem) overnight.'[26] The segregation-desegregation issue is not 'a mere legal one' or 'a moral one'. The Supreme Court decision is a violation causing violence because it does not tackle the American system itself. Faulkner supported 'Gandhi's way' in 1961, and therefore, apparently Martin Luther King's. In fact, Faulkner was no more clear or confused than most Americans in this decade, including those fatalists who, like Lucas Burch, one of Faulkner's Judas figures, believed in agency:

> It seemed to him that they were all just shapes like chessmen—the negro, the sheriff, the money, all—unpredictable and without reason moved here and there by an Opponent who could read his moves before he made them and who created spontaneous rules which he and not the Opponent must follow. . . .

Law, Justice and Justification in William Faulkner

Light in August is a novel of discipline and punishment, in which anxiety over law and order is covered by a required and invented 'rule of certainty'.[27] Faulkner's major mockery and parody of this rule is his fictions of the Snopes clan. A few instances must suffice here, but the relationship of Snopeses to law and justice demands a book to itself.

With the Snopes, Faulkner demonstrates that 'community', 'loyalty' and 'disloyalty' are sites without *inherent* social value, and certainly, like 'sincerity', operate without the law. The dynastic force of these grotesques of 'the family romance' parody the legitimate Jefferson families—Sutpens, Compsons, McCaslins. Their compromising of Major de Spain financially and sexually is a key Faulkner instance of the fragility of morality as a basis of law. But he manages a series of sardonic laughs even though his strategies of humour expose Snopes inieviability. Before them, Will Varner's parcelling out of land into 'small shiftless mortgaged farms for the directors of Jefferson banks to squabble over' (*The Hamlet* (1940)) parodies the 'curse' of land transaction in Yoknapatawpha. Varner 'was a farmer, a usurer, a veterinarian. . . . He held most of the good land of the country and held mortgages on most of the rest.' Rule by Commerce governs and needs no moral conscience.

Mink's motivation of revenge against Flem's betrayal is raw justice (*The Mansion*, 1959, Chapter 12)—'which freedom entitled him to'. Like the convicts in *The Wild Palms* 'he is consumed with outrage and in prison prepared for' the privacy of freedom. His revolver therefore becomes the instrument of an avatar of the Player: 'Old Moster jest punishes; he don't play jokes.' The moment of rough justice once again combines with timeless space:

> *Old Moster don't play jokes* and cocked and steadied the pistol again in both hands, his cousin not moving at all now though he was chewing faintly again, as though he too was watching the dull point of light on the cock of the hammer when it flicked away
>
> It made a tremendous sound though in the same instant Mink no longer heard it . . . it seemed to him, Mink, that the report of the pistol was nothing but that when the chair finished falling and crashed to the floor, the sound would wake all Jefferson.

William Faulkner: The Yoknapatawpha Fiction

This moment of private justice against the head of the clan, whose control of Jefferson exemplifies its corruption, reaches grotesque fulfilment in *The Town* (1957). Now ambiguous lawless rapacity rules. Flem Snopes gains power over the old vested interests: Major de Spain—landowner, sheriff, mayor, whose barn Ab the first Snopes burnt down, father of Colonel Sartoris Snopes; the lawyer Stevens; V. K. Ratcliff, sewing-machine agent, descendant of fighters against the British, who knows the history and people of the town in detail; and the rest of the heavily stratified structure, from self-deemed aristocratic families to servant and cheap-labour Negro descendants of slaves. Moving up from being poor whites, small traders, odd job men, horse-dealers—the story of Book 4 of *The Hamlet*, 'The Peasants'—they become indestructible, or in Faulkner's inimitable terms, they endure, whatever the methods. They have the western grasp of money, being pragmatic in William James's sense of exercizing 'cash values'. They are adepts of capitalist performances for competition and 'possessive individualism'.[28] Their aim is to become bourgeois. Faulkner's ebullient tracing of their rise is also penetrated with anxiety, since their manipulations become indistinguishable from respected Jefferson practice . . . except that the Snopeses lack a sense of guilt, however small, in the violations of mutual aid. And part of their take-over is erotic. Labove, Oxford (Mississippi) law graduate, called to the bar, exists from teaching school at Frenchman's Bend when he tries and fails to seduce his student, Eula Varner (*The Hamlet*)—later Major de Spain's irresistible mistress and Flem Snopes's wife. . . .

The fields of egotism intercept. Legal and extra-legal deals control. The farcical folktale of capitalism is continually undermined by its own drives. But even Flem Snopes's initial appearance (*The Hamlet*) suggests an existential power at his genesis:

> It was as though the original nose had been left off by the original designer or craftsman and the unfinished job taken over by someone of a radically different school or perhaps by some viciously maniacal humorist or perhaps by one who had had only time to clap into the centre of the face a frantic and desperate warning.

Law, Justice and Justification in William Faulkner

But he becomes superintendant of the municipal power plant, an impotent man at the centre of electric energy. His wife Eula is eighteen years the mistress of the president of the Sartoris Bank, so he naturally becomes vice-president. Other Snopeses are properly named after Mississippi senators—Vardaman, Bilbo—or Montgomery Ward Snopes, after the mail order catalogue firm—or Wallstreet Panic, whose brother is Admiral Dewey Snopes. The Snopeses are representative. In World War I, a Snopes runs a canteen behind the lines with a brothel sideline, returns home to run a store as a front for money from exhibiting dirty postcards on a screen, and, after release from prison, makes a last lucrative shift to Hollywood. I. O. Snopes hires a man to tie his mules to the railroad to collect indemnity from the company when a train runs them down. When the man is killed as well, I. O. believes he legally deserves a share of the widow's life insurance, since he was her husband's employer. The case is not uncharacteristic of swindle and legal exploitation. Byron Snopes moves in closer, becoming book-keeper at the Sartoris Bank, loots it, escapes to El Paso, Texas, takes up with an Indian squaw, and then sends back to Flem 'C.O.D. four half-Snopes half-Apache children'. Clarence Snopes adopts them and trains them as a hunting pack until they are wild enough to be returned to Texas. The underside of legalism is often revenge. Clarence is, in fact, at one point a constable of Frenchman's Bend until 'he made the mistake of pistol-whipping in the name of the Law some fellow that was spiteful and vindictive enough to resent being pistol-whipped'. But this Snopes not unnaturally rises to be state senator and intends to run for Congress. Nothing can stop them except themselves, their own autonomy, their own law. No Dark Diceman appears to intervene into their self-motivations. They *are* the Creditor.

In *The Town* Gavin Stevens—successively private defence lawyer, county attorney and judge—takes Flem to be 'his mortal victorious rival and conqueror'. So he becomes a Snopes recorder in impotent fascination, the guardian of the old order become obsessed observer, repeating the familiar terms of 'outrage', 'intractable' and 'impervious', a language of defeat and despair, however realistic. Flem is not only bank vice-president but a deacon of the Baptist church. Beyond the broad satiric comedy of *The Hamlet*, the trilogy becomes dominated by Stevens's interpretative presence. He shapes into narrative Flem's money and power, and Eula's sexual command, as opposition to social economics, marriage and law, out of prior rules of survival that can only be called *natural*. Faulkner tells the stories as forms of legend and lore, to give them authority through different accounts of accumulative information. The Snopeses constitute a preoccupation within what his Nobel prize speech called 'the verities' of human action.

But Flem, too, reaches stasis. Once he has nothing more to achieve, he cannot even spit. Faulkner distinguishes him from Mink Snopes, a character aligned with the convict in 'Old Man', a human reduction that asks for a measure of compassion rather than rigid conventional judgement. In *The Mansion*, Stevens speaks of 'the poor sons of bitches that have to cause all the grief and anguish they have to cause'. Terms like 'plight' enter the story of any man in helpless isolation. Mink and Eula are part of a certain existential rawness and instinctual life that resists social law. This resistance and that of the other Snopeses' behavioural gestures, together with the behaviour of Major de Spain, and the businessmen and tradesmen who elect him mayor, reduce the court-house to a tourist attraction, a laughing stock. The 'invincible and irrevocably polygamous and bachelor' de Spain leads the changes—for instance, selling the family livery stable of horses to buy 'a red E.M.F. roadster', thereby helping eligibility for office. His life with Eula Snopes is considered not so much law-breaking as—in Chick Mallison's words—'what Uncle Gavin called the divinity of simple unadulterated uninhibited mortal lust which they represented . . . ordained Fate . . . ours the pride that Jefferson would supply the battleground'. Flem uses it as another step up—in Stevens's terms (Chapter 2), 'the whole rigid hierarchy moving intact upward one step. . . . Even to impune him so was indefensible and outrageous and forever beyond the pale of pardon.'

But Faulkner's strategies of dislike of the Snopeses extends to their similarity to other major controllers in his ledgers.

Law, Justice and Justification in William Faulkner

His terms for John Brown and the Marshal reappear for I.O.:

> he looked like John Brown with an ineradicable and unhidable flaw . . . a demagogue's capacity for using people to serve his own appetites, all clouded over with a veneer of culture and religion: the very names of his two sons, Byron and Virgil, were not only instances but warnings.

The epic poet in Faulkner itself enters the erosions of control, and indeed he even briefly entertains that such obsessions with the 'all' might deserve rough justice:

> One day a posse of enraged fathers caught him [I.O.] and a fourteen year-old girl in an empty cotton house and tarred and feathered him out of the county. There had been talk of castration also, though some timid conservative dissuaded them into holding that as a promise against his return.

But immediately such interceptions of promiscuity, economic practices and lynch-law are modified, if not cancelled, by Colonel Sartoris, 'our present banker-honorary colonel' (*The Town*, Chapter 2), enabling Byron to attend business college—out of sentimental Confederate army associations in the family. That is, the whole town and its history is involved in Snopes endurance, and not the least, its Confederate 'honour', as a mask of illegality. Stevens summarizes:

> We would never defend Jefferson from Snopeses, let us then give, relinquish, Jefferson to Snopeses, banker mayor aldermen church and all, so that, in defending themselves from Snopeses, Snopeses must of necessity defend and shield us, their vassals and chattels, too.

Eula acts as the erotic part of the promissory note of mythic repetition, the genatrice:

> . . . not Helen nor Semiramis: Lilith: the one before Eve herself whom earth's Creator had perforce in desperate and amazed alarm in person to efface, remove, obliterate, that Adam might create a progeny to populate it. . . .

Stevens's main job inserts Faulkner's functional humour:

> to keep [the Snopes story] from being as funny as it really was, because if he ever let it be as funny as it really was, everybody and himself too would be laughing so hard they couldn't hear him.

But this city attorney is himself a farce:

> it was like watching somebody's britches falling down while he's got to use both hands trying to hold up the roof: you are sorry it is funny, ashamed you had to be there watching.

So Lilith is hilarious, and the trial of Mink Snopes in Chapter 4 a courtroom farce. Stevens has to charge the mayor, his boss, with 'malfeasance in office and criminal connivance', over the power-house case. In fact, this trial breaks up in laughter. To insert at this point the familiar liturgy—'it's for us to cope, to resist; us to endure, and (if we can) survive'—is to ridicule the Nobel prize speech eight years earlier. Faulkner has one last blast at religion to seal in the absurdity.

In Chapter 19, the town's religious controllers—Aryan Baptists, Methodists, Episcopals, Presbyterians, a Chinese laundryman and his family and two Jews—contribute to a chaos, not escaping 'from the tyranny as they claimed and believed, but to establish one'. Farce is eminently a series of rapid and interlinked motions within a static scene—or in Sartre's words in his early and penetrating reading of Faulkner (in 1938 and 1939): 'nothing to come from the future . . . everything has arrived.' But he adds:

> We live in a time of impossible revolution, and Faulkner uses his extraordinary art to describe this world dying of old age and our own suffocation. I admire his art, I do not believe his philosophy: an obstructed future is still a future.[29]

But the long dying culture remains, that clinging refusal abruptly given by Chick Mallison in *Intruder in the Dust*: 'Is: Indivisible.' In the *Faulkner-Cowley File* it is even sharper: 'Mississippi is still the frontier . . . an officer of the law can't go around without a gun where he can reach it fast because he never knows when he's going to need it.' The story emerges from the historical location—'Myth grows spiral-wise . . . it closely corresponds, in the realm of the spoken word, to a crystal in the realm of physical matter' (Claude Lévi-Strauss).

Law is never a neutral term; it has continually to be interrogated and demonstrated. Faulkner's fiction does precisely this, and discovers that the delineatory vocabulary of law can only be exposed in stories, what the courts reduce to cases in order to adjudicate. Legalists claim that Law must ignore time and location, and produce its ledgers of precedent as a static order. Challenges to its abstractions must continue. In the words of Gillian Rose's highly useful analysis, *Dialectical Nihilism*:

> Unaddressable oppositions between morality and legality, autonomy and heteronomy, the good will and natural desire and inclination, force and generality, can be traced to an historically specific legal structure which establishes and protects absolute property by means of the juridical fiction of persons, things and obligations.[31]

Faulkner's fictions dramatize moral conscience at odds with socially established law. Justice is exposed as a term defined in action by energies which are not necessarily legal in local and historical precedents. So a myth of justice examples has to be presented. But the collisions between these forces, and their overwhelming location of justification by religion, political and economic control, and sexuality reduce law and justice to farce, a ridicule which immediately has to be redeemed by reference to a universal co-ordinator, the Creditor and his Board. But it cannot be, and so the stories continue, and their prose has to do the job of coherence. In 1888 Nietzsche noted—he was thinking about the strife between art and truth—'we have art in order not to perish from truth.' If 'truth' includes urges towards inertia and injustice that Faulkner discovered early in his career—it is practically all there in 'A Justice' (*These Thirteen*, 1931)—then his art is a main order against nihilism, the will to power that produces chaos. He created forms and styles to hold stories of conflict and inertia, a poetics to convert intolerable truth into art, 'a new interpretation of sensuousness and the raging discord between art and truth',[32] an heroic enterprise that concluded in the farcical corruption of Jefferson under Snopeses, analogue of so much of the West in Faulkner's lifetime.

William Faulkner: The Yoknapatawpha Fiction

NOTES

1. Robert A. Jellife (ed.), *Faulkner at Nagano* (Tokyo: Kenyusha, 1956), p. 42.
2. W. Y. Tindall, *Forces in Modern British Literature 1885–1956* (New York: Vintage, 1956), p. 140.
3. William Faulkner, *'The Marble Faun' and 'A Green Bough'* (New York: Random House; London: Chatto and Windus, 1967).
4. William Faulkner, *New Orleans Sketches* (London: Brown, Watson, 1961).
5. Susan Willis, 'The Aesthetics of the Rural Slum: Contradictions and Dependency in "The Bear" ', *Social Text*, Vol. 1, No. 2 (Summer 1979), 87.
6. Ernest Hemingway, *A Farewell to Arms* (1929), chapter 34.
7. Gilles Deleuze and Félix Guattari, *Anti-Oedipus: Capitalism and Schizophrenia* (New York: Viking Press, 1977).
8. F. L. Gwynn and J. Blotner (eds.), *Faulkner in the University* (New York: Vintage, 1965), pp. 72–3.
9. Eric Mottram, ' "Thought is always prior to fact": An Introduction', D. K. Adams and I. A. F. Bell (eds.), *American Literary Landscapes* (London: Vision Press; New York: St. Martin's Press, 1988), p. 9.
10. *Faulkner at Nagano*, p. 42..
11. Jean-François Lyotard, *The Post-Modern Condition* (Manchester: Manchester University Press, 1984), pp. 26–7.
12. *Faulkner at Nagano*, p. 188—on the super-power conflict: 'I do not believe they are two ideologies', etc.
13. Alfred Kazin, *On Native Grounds* (London: Cape, 1943), p. 462.
14. Eric Bentley, *A Century of Hero-Worship* (Boston: Beacon Press, 2nd edn., 1957).
15. Perry Miller, *The Life of the Mind in America* (New York: Harcourt, Brace and World, 1965), p. 248.
16. Malcolm Cowley, *The Faulkner-Cowley File* (London: Chatto and Windus, 1966), p. 113.
17. Edmund Leach (ed.), *The Structural Study of Myth and Totemism* (London: Tavistock Publications, 1967), p. 127.
18. J. L. Fant and R. Ashley (eds.), *Faulkner at West Point* (New York: Random House, 1964), p. 103.
19. Frances Yates, *The Art of Memory* (London: Routledge and Kegan Paul, 1966).
20. *The Faulkner-Cowley File*, p. 112.
21. William Empson, *The Structure of Complex Words* (London: Chatto and Windus, 1951), p. 104.
22. *Writers at Work: The Paris Review Interviews* (London: Secker and Warburg, 1958).
23. C. G. Jung, *Symbols of Transformation* (London: Routledge & Kegan Paul, 1956), pt. 2, Chapter VI, 'The Battle of Deliverance from the Mother'.

Law, Justice and Justification in William Faulkner

24. *Faulkner at Nagano*, pp. 98–9.
25. *Faulkner at West Point*, p. 83; *Faulkner at Nagano*, pp. 4 ff.
26. J. B. Meriwether (ed.), *William Faulkner: Essays, Speeches and Public Letters* (London: Chatto and Windus, 1967), p. 37.
27. Michel Foucault, *Discipline and Punish* (London: Allen Lane, 1977), p. 95.
28. C. B. Macpherson, *The Political Theory of Possessive Individualism* (Oxford: Oxford University Press, 1962).
29. Jean-Paul Sartre, *Literary Essays* (New York: Philosophical Library, 1957).
30. *The Faulkner-Cowley File*, p. 110.
31. Gillian Rose, *Dialectical Nihilism: Post-Structuralism and Law* (Oxford: Basil Blackwell, 1984), p. 2.
32. Martin Heidegger, *Nietzsche*, Vol. 1—see: David F. Krell, 'Art and Truth in Raging Discord: Heidegger and Nietzsche on the Will to Power', William V. Spanos (ed.), *Martin Heidegger and the Question of Literature* (Bloomington: Indiana University Press, 1979).

5

Carnival Yoknapatawpha: Faulkner's *Light in August*

by DAVID TIMMS

1

Two questions have predominated in the critical discussion of *Light in August* (1932). The first concerns itself with the relationship between the central figures of the book and the society with which they relate, or fail to relate. It asks what the novel has to say not only about Jefferson as a Southern community, transposed as it was from Faulkner's own Oxford, Mississippi; but also what it has to say about community in general, for which Jefferson might be said to stand as a paradigm. The second is about the unity of the book: is it cohesive as an imaginative whole or do Faulkner's well-known interests and obsessions intrude to a point where the narrative risks fissures and splits? Since the first question is thematic, and the second formal, they appear essentially separate, but seeing each in the light of the other might illuminate both.

In the matter of community the division of opinion has been radical. For Cleanth Brooks in *William Faulkner: The Yoknapatawpha Country* (1963)[1] *Light in August* argues the necessity of community, which operates as a bulwark against disfiguring isolation. 'In *Light in August*', claims Brooks, 'Faulkner's emphasis is primarily on the distortion and perversion and sterility which isolation from the

Carnival Yoknapatawpha: Faulkner's 'Light in August'

community entails.'[2] A counter view is expressed in an important recent essay by André Bleikasten.[3] For him, *Light in August* delineates a society ridden with religious, sexual and racial fanaticism, determined to preserve a white male Protestant hegemony at the price of any act, even murder. Yoknapatawpha, he argues, depends upon 'rigid divisions and arbitrary exclusions . . .'; it is 'a *closed* society, regulated by immutable taboos and demanding from its members total subjection to its law'.[4] Faulkner's view, according to Bleikasten, is Nietzschean, picturing the cultural systems of Yoknapatawpha as systems of cruelty.

Both sides of the argument have faults and virtues. Brooks has a clear political affiliation: he extols the conservative values generated by long attachment to one geographical region. This leads him to distortions: the very title of his chapter on *Light in August*, 'The Community and the Pariah', reverses the foreground and the background of the novel. Moreover, he fails to point to elements in the book that disvalue the community. When the narrator of the book tells us about the crowd that gathers at the site of the burning Burden house, the distaste for the citizens is open. Their sensationalist view of the events:

> . . . made nice believing. Better than the shelves and the counters filled with longfamiliar objects bought, not because the owner desired them or admired them, could take any pleasure in the owning of them, but in order to cajole or trick other men into buying them at a profit.[5]

Similarly the narrator's conjectures about the 'hookworm-ridden heirs at large' (402) who would be the inheritors of Doane's Mill, whence Lena Grove starts her journey, hardly show the community in a shining light. In the same vein Brooks's acceptance that 'there is a clear recognition of a heroic element in Hightower, Joanna Burden, and Joe Christmas',[6] the 'pariahs' against whom the community is ranged, is too grudging. Brooks also has problems with the killing of Joe Christmas, problems betrayed by his attempts to claim that it is a murder not a lynching.[7] To concede that it is a lynching would acknowledge its communal status. Then, too, his blithe claim that this book of horrors is formally the kind of work appropriate for a celebration of community, a pastoral comedy, even if it is so only 'finally and generally',[8] looks too simple by half.

In like manner, it can be said that Bleikasten's non-recognition of the smiling aspects of *Light in August* is equally incomplete. Individuals like the furniture dealer who concludes the book represents the community as surely as the pathological Percy Grimm. Lena Grove is treated with generosity, even if it is sometimes disapproving; certainly hers is not a wholly Nietzschean world. Bleikasten, further, is unwilling or unable to see the jokes and skeins of irony that abound in the discourses of the characters and the narrator, and in the situations and structure of the plot itself. Overall, for both critics, the problem ultimately lies in the urge to see the book's treatment of the community in terms of a single overall explanatory theory, either for or against community values. Both see the community of Jefferson in too abstract a way entirely.

On the rhetoric of the book there is again a split, with further subdivisions. Is it unified or not? And if not, is that good or bad? Early criticism suggested it was a flawed masterpiece. For Richard Rovere in the *Modern Library* edition of 1950, *Light in August* comes across as 'looser in form and structure than any of the [other novels by Faulkner] and among the most implausible in plot'.[9] Subsequent criticism, however, has suggested that there is a concealed unity, in terms of themes or of symbolism. Typical of the latter is C. Hugh Holman's attempt to trace a unifying network of Christian symbols, centred inevitably on Joe Christmas.[10] Still later criticism, influenced by Bakhtin,[11] suggests that the disunity is actually 'polyphony', a modernistic rejection of 'monologism', which involves readers rather than passivizing them. A new essay by Martin Kreiswirth on the relationship between the 'plots and counterplots' of the novel exemplifies this view. He points to:

> ... the wholly dialogical and thus indeterminate nature of the text's ordering of materials. The different narratives cannot come together but can only keep each other, as it were, in line; through a carefully orchestrated process of mutual subversion and deconstruction, the reader repeatedly experiences ... and

Carnival Yoknapatawpha: Faulkner's 'Light in August'

unstable horizons of expectation and, more importantly, the vanishing points of those horizons.[12]

This view of the rhetoric of the text cuts through some of the problems that give rise to the division typified by Brooks and Bleikasten. Since there is no unitary narrative line or point of view centring on an individual character, no 'side' is taken, for or against the community.

Kreiswirth's account is surely accurate, but needs to have more made of it. He deals with the logic of plot and reader expectation, but there is also the matter of narrative voice. Bakhtin himself stresses that *'a genuine polyphony of fully valid voices is in fact the chief characteristic'*[13] (Bakhtin's emphasis) of novels like Dostoevsky's, or, as Kreiswirth suggests, Faulkner's. The chief 'voice' this must affect is that of the omniscient narrator, where a particular novel employs one, since in such novels the convention has it that this voice has a transcendent validity in a hierarchy of discourses. Colin McCabe has called this a 'metalanguage'.[14]

The status of the 'metalanguage' clearly depends not on the truth of the statements themselves but on the conclusiveness of the rhetoric. The absolute knowledge of omniscient narrators about the worlds of their stories stands as guarantee of any comments they might make about the world outside the story. But more important, the consistency of the narratorial voice, its very balance and impersonality, persuades us that it is 'naturally' the voice of common sense. In *Light in August*, however, there are immense variations in the style of the narrator's discourse, in terms of vocabulary and tone. Sometimes he is poetical, using the notorious run-together words that provoked James Agate in an early British review to describe the book as 'precioussilly'.[15] This is normally permissible within a narrator's discourse: he is after all writing something that claims to be 'art'. But we do expect these narrators to be 'well-spoken'. Faulkner's narrator however often uses the colloquial language of the community he describes. We are told of Lucas Burch when he first arrives at the Mill that 'he worked some, though, after a fashion', (426) and Hightower's wife's face was 'thin and gaunted' (444). This process also works in reverse; if on occasions the narrator speaks like the characters, so on occasions the characters sometimes speak like a narrator, using the 'poetic' speech that is normally the narrator's proper province:

> But she don't know yet, no more than she knowed yesterday when she got down from that wagon on the square. Swolebellied, getting down slow from that strange wagon, among them strange faces, telling herself with a kind of quiet astonishment, only I don't reckon there was any astonishment in it, because she had come slow afoot and telling never bothered her: 'My, my. Here I have come clean from Alabama, and now I am in Jefferson at last, sure enough.' (473)

Byron Bunch is here almost quoting words used earlier by the narrator.

The narrator also switches in and out of his characters' language and consciousnesses, sometimes but not always indicating his movement by the use of italics (significantly unbounded by conventional punctuation); but even then he uses a language that is not the language of the character in question:

> She thinks of herself as already moving, riding again, thinking. *Then it will be as if I were riding for a half mile before I even got into the wagon, before the wagon even got to where I was waiting, and that when the wagon is empty of me again it will go on for a half mile with me still in it* She waits, not even watching.... (404)

It should perhaps be noted that in his seminal theoretical work on *The Rhetoric of Fiction* Wayne Booth puts an alternative point of view, using an example from *Light in August* itself. He quotes a passage describing Hightower where, he claims, Faulkner's narrator seems to be making conjectural suggestions about the meaning of what is being described:

> This device may for some readers serve general realistic demands—it is 'as if' the author really shared the human condition to the extent of not knowing for sure how to evaluate these events. But morally the effect is still a rigorous control over the reader's own range of judgement.[16]

In fact, however, Booth's case only holds good in relation to parts of the novel extracted for analysis, for he falsely makes the assumption that the narrator in the novel overall takes

Carnival Yoknapatawpha: Faulkner's 'Light in August'

the conventional stance. Where there is no constant point of origin for the discourse of the narrator, there can be no claim to 'authority'. While we can on many occasions say that the voice we are hearing is not that of one of the characters, we can never say with certainty that it is the same voice we heard when we were last able to describe the text that way. Given the nature of Faulkner's narrator within the polyphony of voices that make up the text, then, no 'authoritative' position is adopted. Faulkner's complex use of his narrator's discourse, his version of indirect free speech, and his manipulation of characters' points of view define his 'polyphony'.

Explaining the rhetoric as 'polyphony', however, does not explain the extraordinary conflict of tones at the end of the book. The lynching is a clear point of conclusion to the central narrative thread of the book and is followed by chapters dealing with events that tie up the other two others: Hightower's reverie and the further progress of Lena. But these final chapters of *Light in August* are not marked by the tone one might normally expect to follow such horrific events: the kind of bleak exhaustion at the end of, say, *King Lear*. Primarily the tone *is* pastoral: this polyphony provides not dissonance but some kind of harmony. And all three conclusions sound a note that is close to Brooks's affirmation: Joe rises 'soaring' into the memories of his murderers and to remain there 'serene' and 'triumphant' (743); Hightower's vision releases some 'ultimate dammed flood' (763) in him that allows his memories of his Grandfather to charge off into the distance; Lena Grove indomitably pursues her career and Byron Bunch comically but loyally supports her. Neither the balance of positive and negative on the subject of the community nor the explanation of the rhetoric of the text as a medley of non-harmonious voices explains the conjunction of cruelty and horror with this dominant tone of pastoral.

2

Let us, then, take Kreiswirth's suggestions about Bakhtin further. The ending of *Light in August* seems a sort of formal culmination because it fulfils requirements of a convention which Bakhtin calls 'carnivalesque'.[17] Carnival literature, according to Bakhtin, provides not simply a rhetoric as described in Kreiswirth's article, but a view of the world. This view is based on the principle of dualism:

> All the images of carnival are dualistic; they unite within themselves both poles of change and crisis: birth and death (the image of pregnant death), blessing and curse (benedictory carnival curses which call simultaneously for death and rebirth), praise and abuse, youth and old age, top and bottom, face and backside, stupidity and wisdom. Very characteristic for carnival thinking is paired images, chosen for their contrast (high/low, fat/thin etc.) or for their similarity (doubles/twins).[18]

This vision is constituted not merely by the plot lines of *Light in August* but by the overall tone of the book, which besides including most of the specific figures alluded to by Bakhtin abides by its overall suggestions. The book generally is an extraordinary mixture of modes. There are strong elements of 'high' drama in Joe Christmas's intense affair with Joanna Burden and its conclusion, but elsewhere equally strong elements of melodrama. When Joe is finally captured in Mottstown and a crazy old man named Hines is returned home to his wife in a state of nervous collapse, his wife asks the old man a question when those who have delivered him have left: 'What did you do with Milly's baby?' (657) And at this point, without waiting for the answer to the most teasing hermeneutic riddle the book has presented us with, the text returns in flashback to the Mottstown square. It might be the stuff of soap opera.

High drama and melodrama at least aspire to the condition of seriousness, but much of this text undermines that intention with humour. There are jokes in names. The insane 'Doc' Hines is really named 'Eupheus', ludicrously suggesting one fair of speech. Joe Christmas is the name of a (potentially black) murderer; Lena is a woman who clearly is not; Hightower is a man who inhabits one; Byron's name is an almost cruel irony. The dialogue is full of jokes. 'I don't recall none named Burch except me, and my name is Bunch' (436) says Byron when Lena first encounters him at the mill, in a piece of dialogue worthy of the Marx Brothers.

There is a great deal of farce. Lena climbs awkwardly

out of her bedroom window and opines that if she had
found it as hard to get out in the first place she might not
be having such difficulty now (403). The hunt for Joe with
the incompetent bloodhounds and their 'apparent infallibility
for metal in any form' (288) is broad slapstick; as is Burch's
frustrated desperate self-pitying obsession with his inability
to get his reward. When Joanna Burden's body is discovered
the countryman who finds it sees that if he is not careful the
head will fall off as he removes the corpse from the burning
building. In the event he succeeds, mainly, but when he puts
the body down he finds Joanna is facing backwards: 'If she
could just have done that when she was alive, she might not
have been doing it now' (466). Brooks sees this very episode
as an attempt to take a middle line, to 'maintain sanity and
human perspective in a scene of brutality and horror'.[19] But
this mis-states the case: it does not mitigate the horror but
turns it inside out, presenting it in another light, as black
comedy. It is the kind of gruesome slapstick we find in the
films of Hitchcock. There is also much comedy of situation:
the minister's wife is a nymphomaniac; Hightower tries to
be above it all but is dragged into a birth and a death over
a weekend; Bunch the solid and Godfearing man loses his
head in an afternoon; the confusion over the names Bunch
and Burch mixes up two radically different personalities.

These observations already begin to identify some of the
'paired images' that fill the book. Characters as superficially
dissimilar as Hightower and Joe Christmas in fact resemble
each other at many points. They are both personalities inter-
nally split, Hightower in time (between his grandfather and
his present), and Christmas (perhaps) in race. They have
alter egos in Bunch on the one hand and Burch on the
other: Bunch's constancy is a comic version of Hightower's
obsession; Burch's drifting a comic version of Joe's ceaseless
driven movement. Minor characters like Doc Hines and
Simon McEachern bear a clear resemblance to each other. In
Hightower's final reverie he finds that the faces of the two
major dramatis personae of the climax of the book, Joe and
Percy Grimm, each driven in his very different way, fuse with
each other.

Knotting together the three essentially separate strands

of the plot there is a pattern of resemblances. There are obvious parallels between the manner of Joe's birth and that of Lena's baby: Joe's grandmother mixes the two up completely. Joanna Burden has partly Mexican parentage, and Joe's father may have been Mexican rather than black. Even within the experience of an individual character there are repeated tropes: Hines's chase after his errant daughter and McEachern's pursuit of his adoptive son have the same obsessiveness.

The carnival view of the world also makes 'possible the transfer of ultimate questions from the abstractly philosophical sphere . . . to the concretely sensuous plane of images and events',[20] according to Bakhtin. In the case of *Light in August*, it generates the novel's mixture of local and universal, of detailed comment on a particular time and place and also on the general and timeless.

André Bleikasten commends *Light in August* as a 'radiograph of the South in the late twenties and early thirties'.[21] But this is a book very much of the '20s, not the '30s. This is not the rural South of the next decade, of, say, Agee's and Evans's *Let Us Now Praise Famous Men* (1941); the comment about the shopkeeper mentality I quote from the book above indicates that we are firmly in the consumer-orientated '20s, before the Crash and the massive increase in unemployment and poverty that came to Mississippi. Despite Bleikasten's claim that he sees the book as about the particular conditions of the South, a distinctive 'closed' society, he does not deal with specific conditions, but with larger scale concerns: gender, race, religion, severed from time and place. More congenial as his politics may be, they are no less clearly based on an ideology. As a carnival text, the novel is rooted in a particular set of social and historic conditions.

America in the 1920s was in a state of rapid, radical and contradictory change. Harding had called in a campaign speech for a spirit of 'rugged individualism' to drive the business engine of the country, but he was preaching a doctrine that was already being practised in the habits of consumption of the 1920s. It was the decade of the washing-machine and the Model T Ford. Herbert Hoover, in his election address of March 1929, gave a sermon of consumerism: 'we are a happy

Carnival Yoknapatawpha: Faulkner's 'Light in August'

people—the statistics prove it. We have more cars, more bathtubs, oil furnaces, silk stockings, bank accounts than any other people on earth.'[22] The boom of the 1920s was experienced in the South as well as in the industrial centres of the North. Between 1920 and 1930 the total urban population of the South increased by nearly twenty-five per cent.[23]

These elements all find expression in *Light in August*. Mississippi was the most rural state and therefore the poorest during the decade, but the book suggests that it too was in a transition period. In rural areas Yoknapatawpha is largely a mule-drawn culture, but in the towns some people are able to afford motor-cars: Joe and Lucas Burch excite envy when they appear in a new one, bought perhaps by Joanna Burden, perhaps on the profits of their bootleg liquor. Clearly the state is in full employment, however, even if wages are not high. Byron Bunch explains to Lena that there is only one planing mill in Jefferson, but there's a 'right smart' of sawmills (436). Percy Grimm works in a cotton office in the town. Drifters like Burch have no difficulty in getting jobs wherever they end up, even if they are jobs normally done by blacks. I have already quoted the narrator's contemptuous comment about the shopkeeper mentality of the crowd that gathers at the Burden place at the time of the fire. The industry of the area is being propelled by the ready availability of credit. Doane's Mill will use up all the timber and then the machinery will be loaded on to freight cars and moved, though some will be abandoned for it is easier to buy new on 'the installment plan' (402).

Individualism in purchasing power informed other kinds of individuality. The era has become known for a new spirit of sexual liberation, and in the nation at large birth-control practices led to a decline in the birth-rate.[24] Less so in the South, however. While the agitation towards women's emancipation was clearly felt in Faulkner's world (Armstid reflects on women who dip snuff and smoke and want to vote (409)), it was still the case that the population was increasing in that section rather than the reverse.[25] We are told of the yearly augmenting of Lena's sister-in-law's family (402), and that Armstid's wife had had five children in six years (410).

In some regions there was a spirit of experiment about

new forms of government, too, like the New York City administration of Al Smith (which included F. D. Roosevelt), and in the South the Louisiana Government of Huey Long. Even Lucas Burch has felt some of the breeze of new political ideas: despairing about his inability to lay hold of his rights or his money, he complains that the sheriff will not protect 'a American citizen. . . . I be dog if it aint enough to make a man turn downright bowlsheyvick' (723).

But in opposition to these forces for expansion there were equally clear forces for repression. The war had fostered a national dislike of anything 'foreign'. There was a general suspicion of 'hyphenated Americans' which increased during the war, and according to Hugh Brogan

> what may be called the cultural panic of the postwar period expressed itself, as was natural, in noisier and noisier assertions of American superiority and in a dread of foreign infiltration.[26]

This generalized fear, and the agitation of the labour unions over the importation of cheap labour resulted in a series of legislative acts—the Immigration Act (1917), the Quota Act (1921) and the Johnson-Reed Act (1924)—designed to keep the foreigner out. Brogan quotes a representative opinion from Senator Albert Johnson of Washington State:

> The myth of the melting pot has been discredited. . . . The United States is our land. If it was not the land of our fathers, at least it may be, and should be, the land of our children.[27]

W. J. Cash suggested in his celebrated *The Mind of the South* (1941) that this sentiment was felt as strongly in the rest of the South; and one effect of the war was to foster a feeling of common bond with other Americans, even Yankees, against outsiders: '. . . the militant and intolerant Americanism' propaganda by such national confraternities (themselves of course the product and embodiment of the common national fears and hatreds) as the American Legion and the Patriotic Order of Sons of America, with their 'Red Perils' and 'alien menaces', nowhere found more receptive soil than in Dixie.[28]

The most famously repressive legislation of all was of course Prohibition, made law by the Volstead Act of 1919.

This institutional oppression encouraged widespread corruption; it is a historical commonplace that Prohibition and the resultant bootleg liquor industry made organized crime a major feature of American life. Joe Christmas and Lucas Burch of course make their income primarily from the bootleg liquor trade, and not from their efforts at the planing mill. In the South, according to W. J. Cash, local conditions gave Prohibition particular effects, which are significant for *Light in August*. Cash indicates that while the big money was made by the white entrepreneurs, on the ground and particularly in urban environments the bootleg liquor trade was largely in the hands of blacks. Black men tended to operate not only as purveyors of liquor but also as pimps to white prostitutes. In this position they were able to demand sexual favours of the white women, in return for 'protection'.

> The result was the rise of a horde of raffish blacks, full of secret, contemptuous knowledge of the split in the psyche of the shamefaced Southern whites, the gulf between their Puritanical professions and their hedonistic practices—scarcely troubling to hide their grinning contempt for their clients under the thinnest veil of subservient politeness and, in the case of the bellboys, hugging to themselves with cackling joy their knowledge of the white man's women.[29]

Cash was of course himself a Southerner, and whatever its status as historical fact, what the emotional tone of this passage betrays is the intensity of feeling in Southern white men, and the way for the Southerner the bootleg liquor trade was linked with race and sexuality. Joe Christmas's status may thus be seen to be even more problematic in the community of Jefferson: not only an outsider, but one doing a manual job normally associated with blacks, making the bulk of his income from criminal activity normally associated with blacks, and finally, as it transpires, engaged in an activity the very thought of which stirred the most intense paranoia.

These elements of the time then combined into a volatile mixture of legislation designed to prevent change and a ferment of social and economic pressures bound to foster it. The result in economic terms was the Crash of 1929, the banking collapse of 1930 and the depression and unemployment that followed. In social terms the mixture stimulated insecurity and intolerance, the most notorious expression of which was the execution of Sacco and Vanzetti in 1927. During the trial the Judge had referred to them as 'anarchist bastards', but Vanzetti's last statement before his execution asserted that he had suffered 'because I am an Italian', as well as because he was a radical.

Light in August clearly chronicles the results of this fear and intolerance, in Percy Grimm's brutal treatment of Joe Christmas in the name of America, in Christmas's own feeling of alienation at this otherness, in the activities of the Ku Klux Klan members who beat up Hightower owing to rumours about his relationship with his cook. It is expressed in the obvious rabid aggression towards blacks in the beliefs and practices of people like Hines and McEachern, in more sinister form in the way the sheriff routinely beats blacks to obtain information he already knows, and in the suggestion that it is more of an insult to imply that a man is part black than to accuse him of a murder (470).

As a 'carnivalesque' text *Light in August* mixes this direct approach to local social concerns with comment on the most universal of issues. André Bleikasten usefully underscores the point in a description of how the ascendant Yoknapatawpha culture of the novel perpetuates itself:

> Puritanism, sexism, racism. What joins them is obviously more than ideological kinship: a structural homology, an identical functioning. Each of them generates an order by way of distinctions and disjunctions. . . . One divides to oppose: ideal versus real, male versus female, white versus black. One term in a binary opposition is always valued over the other. Whereas ideality, masculinity, and whiteness are exalted, their opposites are abased. To divide is to pass judgement, to name the categories of good and evil, to assign them to fixed locations, and to draw between them boundaries not to be crossed. On the good side, *inside*, the clear, clean, orderly space of all that is valuable; on the other, *outside*, the alien, enemy territories of darkness and disorder, the abject kingdom of evil.[30]

As a broad view of the Southern modes of thinking evident in *Light in August* this analysis seems to me extremely persuasive. Bleikasten himself notes that what outrages the people of Mottstown when Joe is captured is not that he is a murderer, or that as a black man he has had sexual relations with a white woman, but that 'he never acted like either a nigger or white man. That was it. That was what made the folks so mad' (658).

In *Purity and Danger* (1966) Mary Douglas offers a statement which anticipates Bleikasten's view of culture:

> I believe that ideas about separating, purifying, demarcating and punishing transgressions have as their main function to impose system on an inherently untidy experience. It is only by exaggerating the difference between within and without, above and below, male and female, with and against, that a semblance of order is created.[31]

Douglas suggests that in many cultures there are rituals to reinforce or to introduce notions of wholeness and distinctness, in which power is seen to reside: in Judaism for instance 'Holiness is the attribute of Godhead. Its root means "set apart".'[32] Social stability is often symbolized by bodily integrity, which is why in so many cultures there are complex rules about what can enter or leave the body and in what circumstances. Joe Christmas is ironically a paradigm member of his (white) culture in his anxiety about preserving this integrity. He associates danger with the transgression of his bodily margins, as when he links the episode of the eating of the toothpaste with his departure from the orphanage, or will not eat with Byron Bunch when he first comes to the mill ('Keep your muck' (424)), or rejects the food offered to him by Joanna, smashing the plates against the wall. The episode when he refuses to learn McEachern's catechism can be seen in the same way, as a refusal to 'take in' a creed. He feels safest with what is clear and hard-edged, and therefore, though he has experienced only cruelty from men, feels uneasy with the traditionally feminine as opposed to the masculine.

But in spite of his intentions he lives always at the margins, and this marginality is stressed throughout the book, in literal and metaphorical ways. When he comes to Jefferson Joe actually lives at the edge of the town, and at the edge of the Burden household. Joanna 'had never invited him inside the house proper' (571), only into the kitchen: the kitchen then is the margin of the house. Before he murders Joanna he walks from Jefferson into Freedmantown, the black quarter, and back, in the margin of the two societies. On the run he loses all sense of boundaries: even 'Time, the spaces of light and dark, had long since lost orderliness' (291). He even loses the sense of what is edible and what is not, for when he is on the run he eats rotten food and uncooked food, which give him 'crises of bleeding flux' (292): unable to control his outflows as well as his ingestion, losing his sense of his physical boundaries. Thus he cannot be put in one category or the other, and as a case that the rules do not seem to fit he is a living challenge not only to the rules, but to the very idea of rules.

3

I suggested above that Bleikasten's response to *Light in August* is contradictory since he praises the book as a 'radiograph' of the South, but takes no account of the detail of this radiograph. He does not apply his own perception. Something similar might be said of his treatment of the universals in the book. Bleikasten wants to draw distinctions between societies, not simply to describe how societies function. If Faulkner's South is a 'closed' society, there must be possible societies that are 'open'. His answer is to make a suggestion about group psychology. The culture of Faulkner's South, he suggests, is

> a collective neurosis as all cultures are . . . the Puritan culture dramatized in Faulkner's novel originates in and is based on repression. What sets it apart is that the amount of repression exacted is exceptionally high.[33]

The problem with this is that it exemplifies the very view of the world that it criticizes: societies are either open or closed, one thing or the other, either this side of the margin or that. Bleikasten's is in fact a 'closed' view, on his own terms, and the mark of it is that inability to see the positive elements of Faulkner's picture of his society that I comment on above. As Bakhtin makes clear, the carnival world view is one that obscures all margins, making it possible for events and characters to have a comic face and a tragic, a good side and a bad, and for both to be evident simultaneously.

Joe's lynching obviously performs a function for the community. Mary Douglas explains that 'Holiness requires that individuals shall conform to the class to which they belong. And holiness requires that different classes of things shall not be confused.'[34] The particular 'holy' value being asserted by Percy Grimm is the integrity of the community. The lynching of Joe Christmas clears up any confusion: he must be black, because only blacks are lynched. (A certain tribe, according to Mary Douglas, preserve their definition of a cock as a bird that crows at dawn by throttling any cock that crows at another time.') Mary Douglas suggests that

> since place in the hierarchy of purity is biologically transmitted, sexual behaviour is important for preserving the purity of caste. For this reason, in higher castes, boundary pollution focuses primarily on sexuality.[35]

The castration of Joe perfects the ritual, and Grimm's very act of separating and defining, in the literal and metaphorical senses, itself exemplifies the values he kills for: order not confusion.

But within the patterns of the book the treatment given to this supposed black murderer has clear suggestions of Christian sacrifice about it, both serious and parodic. Joe's surname reminds us of his sacrificial rôle, and we are told that the crowd that gathers at the Burden house are 'looking for someone to crucify' (612). On the other hand Percy Grimm's butchering is a Grand Guignol version of Christ's being speared in the side. The formal links are to be sure those given attention in the article by C. Hugh Holman cited earlier. But it is important to note that the suggestions are not enough to make a straightforward identification between Joe and Christ; it is equally important to stress that the inexactness of the fit (for instance, the fact that Joe is 36 at the time of his death, not 33, the age of Christ at the crucifixion; or that his name is 'Christmas', not 'Easter'). Which is not to invalidate their status as *suggestions*. Once again, the attempts of some to see Joe as Christ, and the attempts of others to deny it by pointing to detail in both cases is to take all or nothing, the one or the other view that carnival literature expressly undermines.

It is thus extremely tempting to see the town square of Jefferson, where the scene that culminates in Joe's lynching begins, as a version of the carnival square, which according to Bakhtin 'glimmers' in carnival literature 'behind almost all scenes and events of real life, most of which are portrayed in a naturalistic manner'. The carnival square has 'its specific carnival logic of familiar contacts, mesalliances, disguises and mystifications, contrasting paired images, and so forth'.[36] Equally, Joe's death may be seen as the carnival decrowning that Bakhtin identifies as the primary carnivalistic act.[37] The event has the resonance of symbol which works by suggestion, being both alike and different at once, not simply on the epistemological level, but on the emotional level too.

In the penultimate chapter of *Light in August* Hightower has a vision that culminates in 'some ultimate dammed flood within him' (763) breaking and rushing away, something like the 'pent black blood' (743) which rushes out of Joe's pale body. Visions can be said to work in a similar way to ritual events; dreams and trances are states in which we perceive truths that our conscious minds cannot reach, rather as rituals are symbolic enactments that express belief and feelings that can never be wholly articulated. Hightower's vision does not clarify things: the very reverse, for all the figures in his vision 'look a little alike', even though 'he can distinguish them'. Joe's face is not clear, however, for 'it is two faces which seem to strive . . . in turn to free themselves one from another, then fade and blend again' (762–63). His recognition that the other element in the composite face is the face of the man who killed Joe is the signal for the breaking of the 'dammed flood'. Hightower recognizes the fact that what is inside the margin is defined by what is outside it; there is no absolute distinction such as Grimm's act was intended to enforce: the distinction is relative.

Similarly with the very last chapter of the book: Joe has been 'replaced' by Lena's baby, and though Lena says that she is still in pursuit of his father, we have no doubt, like the furniture dealer, that it will not be long before Bunch replaces Burch. Carnival literature, according to Bakhtin, is not about

Carnival Yoknapatawpha: Faulkner's 'Light in August'

absolutes but relationships and shifting meanings:

> Carnival celebrates the shift itself, the very process of replaceability, and not the precise item that is Carnival is, so to speak, functional and not substantive. It absolutizes nothing, but rather proclaims the joyful relativity everything.[38]

It is the carnival view that informs technique and meaning in *Light in August*, and gives it such great pliability as a text—a story at once epic, horrific, comic and pastoral.

NOTES

1. Cleanth Brooks, *William Faulkner: The Yoknapatawpha Country* (New Haven and London: Yale University Press, 1963).
2. Brooks (1963), p. 70.
3. André Bleikasten, '*Light in August*: The Closed Society and its Subjects', in Michael Millgate (ed.), *New Essays on 'Light in August'* (London: Cambridge University Press, 1987, pp. 81–102).
4. Bleikasten (1987), p. 96.
5. William Faulkner, *Light in August* (1932), in *Novels 1930–1935* (New York: Library of America, 1985), p. 612. Future references will be made in brackets in the text.
6. Brooks (1963), p. 70.
7. See Brooks's comments on p. 52 of *William Faulkner: The Yoknapatawpha Country*, and his note on 'The "Lynching" of Joe Christmas', p. 377.
8. P. 71.
9. Richard H. Rovere, 'Introduction', *Light in August* (New York: The Modern Library, 1950), p. vi.
10. C. Hugh Holman, 'The Unity of Faulkner's *Light in August*', *P.M.L.A.*, 73 (March 1958), 155–66.
11. See Mikhail Bakhtin, *Problems of Dostoevsky's Poetics*, ed. Caryl Emerson (Manchester: University of Manchester Press, 1984).
12. Martin Kreiswirth, 'Plots and Counterplots: The Structure of *Light in August*', in Millgate (1987), p. 77.
13. Bakhtin (1984), p. 6.
14. Colin McCabe, 'Realism and the Cinema', *Theoretical Essays: Film, Linguistics, Literature* (Manchester: Manchester University Press, 1985), p. 37.
15. Quoted by Michael Millgate, 'Introduction', in Millgate (1987), p. 14.
16. Wayne C. Booth, *The Rhetoric of Fiction* (Chicago and London: University of Chicago Press, 1961), p. 184.
17. See 'Characteristics of Genre and Plot Composition in Dostoevsky's Works', in Bakhtin (1984), pp. 101–80.

18. Bakhtin (1984), p. 126.
19. Brooks (1963), p. 71.
20. Bakhtin (1984), p. 134.
21. Bleikasten (1987), p. 99.
22. Quoted in Peter N. Carroll and David W. Noble, *The Free and the Unfree: A New History of the United States* (London: Penguin Books, 1977), p. 335.
23. See W. J. Cash *The Mind of the South* (1941; London: Penguin Books, 1973), p. 273.
24. See Carr and Noble (1977), p. 320.
25. See Cash (1941), p. 287.
26. Hugh Brogan, *The Pelican History of the United States of America* (London: Penguin Books, 1986), p. 511.
27. Brogan (1986), p. 512.
28. Cash (1941), p. 305.
29. Cash (1941), p. 322.
30. Bleikasten (1987), p. 96.
31. Mary Douglas, *Purity and Danger: An Analysis of the Concepts of Pollution and Taboo* (1966; London: Ark Books, 1984), p. 4.
32. Douglas (1966), p. 49.
33. Bleikasten (1987), p. 92.
34. Douglas (1966), p. 53.
35. Douglas (1966), p. 125.
36. Bakhtin (1984), p. 133.
37. Bakhtin (1984), p. 124.
38. Bakhtin (1984), p. 125.

6
Marking Out and Digging In: Language as Ritual in *Go Down, Moses*

by GRAHAM CLARKE

> In the beginning it was virgin—to the west, along the Big River, the alluvial swamps threaded by black almost motionless bayous and impenetrable with cane and buckvine and cypress and oak and gum; to the east, the hardwood ridges and the prairies where the Appalachian mountains died and buffalo grazed; to the south, the pine barrens and the moss-hung liveoaks and the greater swamps less of earth than water and lurking with alligators and water moccasins, where Louisiana in its time would begin.
> —William Faulkner, 'Mississippi' (1954)[1]

> Go down, Moses,
> Way down in Egyptland
> Tell old Pharaoh
> To let my people go.
> —'Negro' spiritual[2]

1

Yoknapatawpha county remains basic to any sense of the Faulkner achievement. That 'little postage stamp of earth' modelled upon Oxford and Lafayette County, Mississippi, establishes itself not just as background to the novels, nor just as locality, but as a distinct presence against which we judge the history and lives of Faulkner's Southern individuals. As Malcolm Cowley insisted in his introduction to *The Portable Faulkner* (1946), Faulkner wanted 'to invent a Mississippi county that was like a mythical kingdom . . . and to make his story of Yoknapatawpha county stand as a parable and legend of all the Deep South'.[3]

And yet *Go Down, Moses*, whilst it is saturated with the presence of Yoknapatawpha, has a peculiar status in relation to the larger cycle of Yoknapatawpha texts. To begin with it comes after what we might view as the major Yoknapatawpha novels: *Sartoris* (1929), *The Sound and the Fury* (1929), *As I Lay Dying* (1930), *Sanctuary* (1931), *Light in August* (1932), and *Absalom, Absalom!* (1936). In addition it is not a novel, as such, but a collection of seven short stories, seemingly lacking the breadth, and sustained intensity, of the major novels. Indeed, of the seven stories in the cycle ('Was', 'The Fire and the Hearth', 'Pantaloon in Black', 'The Old People', 'The Bear', 'Delta Autumn', and 'Go Down, Moses') only 'The Bear' is usually much known to readers. 'The Bear' has been 'reprinted, anthologised, and discussed' as if it 'constituted an independent entity',[4] even though Faulkner said that he saw the 'stories' as a *novel*.[5] Indeed as a novel *Go Down, Moses* speaks directly to Yoknapatawpha, and makes a Southern landscape basic to its meaning.

I want to argue, however, that *Go Down, Moses* is not just an essential Yoknapatawpha text, but that it both extends and complicates Faulkner's sense of place and of Southernness. In short, I want to suggest that in its singular concern to evoke Yoknapatawpha county *Go Down, Moses* figures place not just in the context of a 'Southern' heritage and history, but in relation to America as a whole. It offers, in other words, a view of the South as an alternative locus for the myth of American meaning. And yet it does so at the level of language and of poetry—for it seeks a verbal weight the equivalent of the land on which Faulkner lays his significance. In its view of the land, and of what is happening to it, it thereby extends a central American tradition concerned with the exploitation of the continent—but, crucially, distinguishes itself from it.

In a text saturated with history it offers a sense of place

Marking Out and Digging In: Language as Ritual

wholly distinct from its East or West Coast equivalents. In 1946 William Carlos Williams published the first volume of *Paterson*, his own great epic of American place. *Go Down, Moses* exists as its precursor—an alternative trope to Williams's attempt to forge a language appropriate to a land seen through the line of Whitman, Thoreau and Emerson. In *Go Down, Moses* Faulkner views America neither through the cultural perspective of New England nor of the West—but through the perspective of his Southern precursor: Edgar Allan Poe, a southern heritage cursed by history and its image on the land.

And yet one of the most prevalent words in *Go Down, Moses* is 'wilderness'—as if Faulkner, literally and symbolically, seeks a wilderness condition, a pristine America as much devoid of cultivation and settlement as did Thoreau. As such *Go Down, Moses* shares its concern with other central texts in American literary tradition likewise concerned with the myth of place, especially that of an original America, but adds to the dualism of Eastern and Western a Southern presence which makes the issue both problematic and ambiguous. The New England attempt to image a new-found land, a Canaan as Emerson suggested in which the American became the new Adam re-naming as he re-discovered and re-stored language via a pristine nature above and outside history, for Faulkner in *Go Down, Moses* is given an alternative interpretation. The New England heritage is essentially a clear-eyed idealism: seeing in the land a transparent clearness. The land, in Thoreau's *Walden* or Emerson's *Nature* exists as a pure image—shot through with God's radiant presence as part of a larger process of being and higher significance. In a similar sense the West offered (and still offers) this ideal condition on a larger scale: at once individual and composite, part of the 'open road' and the 'passage to India' basic to Whitman's sense of the Western spaces as pragmatic, prospective and sublime. In the nineteenth century, certainly, both act as equal integers of American myth (and meaning) and for a poet like Whitman constitute the centre of American significance. History, as such, is transcended. The land, as a native wilderness, symbolizes an ideal state through which the word, via the eye/I of the poet will, as Whitman proclaimed, 'project the history of the future'.

For Faulkner, and especially so in *Go Down, Moses*, the South inverts this trope and gives to a sense of American place an historical perspective which views the culture as implosive rather than expansive. In Edgar Allan Poe as much as Mark Twain this sense of difference is crucial, for the landscape of the South pictures an image of the culture and of the word which not only undercuts and corrodes the pragmatic and ideal paradigms of East and West Coast America, but suggests the South, ultimately, as their dark 'other': a land and heritage emptied of meaning. To invoke a sense of the land, thus, is to make a language itself as corroded as the scene upon which the writer looks.

Go Down, Moses thus complicates Faulkner's sense of American place and gives to Yoknapatawpha, as a focus *and* base for the novels, a distinctive awareness of the land which speaks to the fiction's deepest sense of self and, crucially, of the *word*. In *As I Lay Dying*, for example, we are given one of Faulkner's quintessential statements on the relationship between the land and a particular kind of Southernness:

> That's the one trouble with this country: everything, weather, all, hangs on too long—like our rivers, our land: opaque, slow, violent; shaping and creating the life of man in its implacable and brooding image.[6]

The 'South' is thus pictured as a condition which literally presses down on its inhabitants. And yet *Go Down, Moses* is primarily about loss: the loss of a wilderness condition and of a consciousness felt as its equivalent. 'Man' in the text is not so much viewed as being shaped by the land as by being in constant opposition to it. As such he writes his history on to it and, in so doing, disinherits himself and his children from an original condition. Thus if *Go Down, Moses* is, in part, about the terms on which white settlers attempt to possess the land, making of it consistently a reflection of their power and control, it is equally about dispossession. The 'original' America they obliterate becomes the lost image of their own 'original sin': born of greed and guilt. The South is thus offered as an image which paradoxically reflects Emerson's symbolic terms

Marking Out and Digging In: Language as Ritual

for reading nature; the state of the land is held forth as 'a metaphor of the human mind'.

Faulkner's text, then, pictures the history of American man in his ever-increasing attempt to impose order upon a wilderness condition. Each story suggests a different image of the same process as each 'narrative' is given its significance in place: a land itself the historical text (and map) of man's mis-use and endless corrosive power over a lost 'green world'. Thus, 'this land which so you claim God created and man himself cursed and tainted. Not to mention 1865 . . .'.[7] History here compounds the loss of 'America' as an ideal. All of man's activity has corrupted the land. History becomes a mapping of the possession and exploitation of a wilderness condition. The land, as such, has always been 'corrupted' by man: white and Indian alike. Thus, 'He saw the land already accursed even as Ikkemotubbe and Ikkemotubbe's father old Issetibbeha, and old Issetibbeha's father too held it . . .' (GDM, 197). This sense of corruption, corrosion and dispossession reverberates through *Go Down, Moses* with the force of Old Testament judgement. Indeed, the stories suggest a continuing cycle of disinheritance as pervasive and dominant as Ahab's alienation in his attempt to possess the whale in *Moby-Dick*. The 'hereditary land', in addition, becomes a reflection of both a lost America, and of the condition to which Faulkner's mythic anti-hero of the cycle approaches. Isaac McCaslin achieves benediction to the extent that he 'owned no property'.

And yet around McCaslin swirls a process which, as in *Moby-Dick*, seeks to possess and kill in order to bring the land under direct control. The original sin—the urge to know and order—is offered as a reflection of a dangerous and dislodged Southern American self. But *Go Down, Moses* is no mere polemic. Faulkner pictures this process of deracination as part of an *inner* condition: at once as much paradoxical as it is ultimately insoluble. The urge to possess becomes part of what Faulkner calls 'the heart's driving complexity'. Any rhetoric of American beginnings is displaced by a language of ambiguous and significant limitation: a poetic mapping of a culture's condition. The white Southerners may have 'bought the land, took the land, got the land . . .' (GDM, 155), but they have done so from a position where the 'land is . . . of and by itself cursed' (GDM, 227). The condition is endemic, placing man's attempt to use and control the land against the larger myths of Canaan and Eden:

> The curse you whites brought into this land has been lifted. It has been voided and discharged. We are seeing a new era, an era dedicated, as our founders intended it, to freedom, liberty, and equality for all, to which this country will be the new Canaan. (GDM, 213)

Faulkner does not just inveigh against such a statement as part of a naïve and empty rhetoric; he brings to bear upon it the entire Southern racial history of blacks and whites—evoking a felt sense of prejudice at the level of the subconscious. Indeed the blacks in *Go Down, Moses* exist amidst a continuing legacy of the violent and the brutal: *their* legacy, as 'Go Down, Moses' suggests, is a migration to Northern cities, to be symbolically disinherited as a mere number in a census or executed by electricity. There is no saving grace in *Go Down, Moses*, nor a path of escape. It ends, as McCaslin knows and sees, on an image of emptiness, a vacant interior: a lost heritage in which language, for Faulkner, can only reflect a process whereby wilderness disappears in favour of an alien and unfeeling geometry of control—plantations, roads, and railways. Linear fences and lines of limitation. A white text spewn across the black land.

2

Go Down, Moses, thus, makes the *land* its central image. Far from making marginal human activity on the land, Faulkner insists again and again on how man's actions write themselves on to it—re-inscribing the values (as well as the fears and greeds) of the culture over the surface. As such the evidence, anthropological as much as archaeological, is one of endless exploitation—of black by white, of animal by man, and of land by man. As Ursula Brumm has suggested, *Go Down, Moses* offers a 'wholesale indictment of civilization as rapacious, seeing its best fruits precisely a sublimation of

Marking Out and Digging In: Language as Ritual

this, its innermost nature'.[8] Thus 'Already in *Go Down, Moses* allusion is made to the rapacity of the westward expansion, and the plantation is made symbol of exploitation—on a world-historical scale. . . .'[9]

The constant references throughout the text to a language of ownership, property, title and inheritance underscore this sense of possession. Indeed the opening story ('Was') begins with the language of ownership basic to the conflicts of the stories as a whole. 'Inheritor', 'bequestor', 'title', 'land', 'county' and 'patent', for example, stamp themselves on the initial paragraphs as part of an endemic language of control: a misplaced legal vocabulary in which 'ownership' is vested. As against this Isaac McCaslin 'owned no property and never desired to since the earth was no man's but all men's'. He dispossesses himself in order to return to the land but, like Old Ben, by the end is isolated amidst an unstoppable process of destruction and endless clearance.

Like 'Was' each story inculcates part of a larger history of thwarted and corrupted possession—most obviously in a slave-owning economy—but metaphysically as part of a pervasive drama against which Faulkner views individualism as the basis of a wasteful and fated rapaciousness. The ledgers in which the McCaslin 'story' is held are, thus, not so much a family chronicle as a testament of stolen rights and lost rites. 'The old frail pages' of a file of human misuse and corruption, exist as a

> record which two hundred years had not been enough to complete and another hundred would not be enough to discharge; that chronicle which was a whole land in miniature, which multiplied and compounded was the entire South. . . . (GDM, 224)

But the ledger here is also a text of calculation—a parallel text to the map of activity by which the Southern wilderness is being changed, exploited and cursed. Indeed, the sense of exploitation is as vehement and intense in *Go Down, Moses* as anything in *Moby-Dick*. Ahab's hatred of the whale is seemingly echoed in the Southern response to the land: an economy—most obviously figured in the plantation—based on thwarted energies so deep and basic, as to establish an alternative myth of American expansion, as far from Emerson's individual 'vision' as possible. Thus the ledgers stand for the plantation: tablets of stone almost, on which is written out a chronicle of greed. The ledgers condense

> the whole plantation in its mazed and intricate entirety—the land, the fields and what they represented in terms of cotton ginned and sold . . . that whole edifice intricate and complex and founded upon injustice and erected by ruthless rapacity and carried on even yet with at times downright savagery. . . .
> (GDM, 227)

The plantation thus exists as the visible image of a Southern history, cursed by its urge to own; but it also exists as an image of expansion—of an energy which at once destroys the wilderness in favour of an economic base unrepentant and unconcerned as to its inherent destructive energies. In *Go Down, Moses* this is the consistent way in which Faulkner views the disappearance of a wilderness America. Indeed, a farming culture is associated with a negative vocabulary of order and control—re-writing itself over the land in relation to a culture more obviously associated with Faulkner's view of the North. The clearings for farms, thus, cut through and into an original South—breaking down the circular, organic and holistic wilderness. In its place is left a geometry of possession symptomatic of the culture's way with the world: angular, linear and separate, akin to the obsessive world of Quentin when he is displaced North to Harvard in *The Sound and the Fury*. Equally the extent to which farming is also equated with clearing associates is with an openness symptomatic of an open-eyed (and yet dangerously naïve) view of the world: as much solipsistic as imagistic, for this map of lines and angles assumes a superficial knowledge and control, a symbolic sense of light as against the darkness to which *Go Down, Moses* seeks a return.

In this sense it is absolutely crucial that a distinction is made throughout the stories between a plantation (and farming) culture, and hunting not simply in the way, say, Cooper distinguishes between them in *The Pioneers*, for McCaslin is no Natty Bumppo, but in relation to a sense of self *and* land basic to the condition Faulkner evokes. The significance

Marking Out and Digging In: Language as Ritual

(and essential mystery) of hunting is, for example, made crucial to both 'The Bear' and 'Delta Autumn'. In them hunting is given the status of a primordial act: an agent of initiation into what the wilderness represents as the image of a condition the very opposite of the modern and the 'new', at once ambiguous and mythical. The hunt is part of a larger rite of initiation into the wilderness itself—a metaphor of man's inner and archetypal self: a lost language of being. Its centrality is such that it exists as part of a dark other—bloody and ruthless—to which Northern pragmatism and progress give the lie.

Just as the word 'wilderness' reverberates through the text, so 'dark' is associated with an endless hunt as part of an internal psychic condition Faulkner seeks to invoke. Hunting is thus an ambiguous act—but in a pure sense allows a return to an original state—not of innocence, but of a complex and hidden past. A ritual initiation and re-birth of an archetypal American self: thus the significance of entering the forests to hunt, for they are the locale of the dark other which, in 'The Bear', holds a 'spirit' which can never be caught. 'Old Ben', the bear, is accordingly

> an anachronism indomitable and invincible out of an old dead time, a phantom, epitome and apotheosis of the old wild life which the little puny humans swarmed and hacked at in a fury of abhorrence and fear like pygmies about the ankles of a drowsing elephant—the old bear, solitary, indominatible, and alone. . . . (GDM, 147)

The bear becomes, so to speak, the very image of a wilderness state; for as the 'puny humans' hack at it, so they 'hack' away at the 'doomed wilderness' whose 'edges were being constantly and punily gnawed at by men with ploughs or axes who feared it because it was wilderness . . .' (GDM, 147). As with *Moby-Dick*, so the 'fiery hunt' in *Go Down, Moses* is part of a larger (and savage) devouring of nature—but a nature which echoes back a heartless condition in which man's attempt to achieve a central *place* (the control and order after his own image of self)—is potentially shattered by its overwhelming presence and darkness.

In this sense the young Isaac McCaslin in 'The Bear' is both an initiate to this disfiguring energy as he is a recipient of the wilderness as an incipient presence and opens out to an awareness of the 'other' in which this condition is held. Just as he travels further and further 'into the new and alien country than he had ever been' (GDM, 157), so he travels further, and deeper, into the self—not to exorcize so much as to regain a lost condition:

> By noon he was far beyond the crossing on the little bayou, farther into the new and alien country than he had ever been, travelling now not only by the compass but by the old, heavy, biscuit-thick silver watch which had been his father's. . . . He stood for a moment—a child, alien and lost in the green and soaring gloom of the markless wilderness. Then he relinquished completely to it. It was the watch and the compass. He was still tainted. He removed the linked chain of the one and the looped thong of the other from his overalls and hung them on a bush and leaned the stick beside them and entered it. (GDM, 157–58)

To enter the wilderness, thus, is equivalent to a rite of primogeniture and marks a return to a voiceless condition. Without watch and compass, heavily insistent tokens of his relationship to time and space, order and control which the 'puny' humans impose upon the wilderness, so McCaslin gives himself over to that 'other', an original point of contact with an older America. 'Lost', he is, surrounded by a presence impossible to calculate and make finite. And as he enters it so, amidst its 'soaring gloom', for this is no Eden or Canaan, he reaches a markless spot. In a text full of the endless evidence of human movement and mapping: of marks, mounds, tracts, prints, lines, walls, fences, roads, and railways, so he reaches an original America—but one sombre, dark, and silent—not, as for Emerson and Whitman, light and clear. At such a point of entry, so he regains re-entry into a lost self. At such a moment so 'it seemed to him' that 'he was witnessing his own birth'.

The wilderness, then, 'the big woods, bigger and older than any recorded document—of white man fatuous enough to believe he had bought any fragment of it' (GDM, 145) is the depository with which Faulkner's text seeks cognizance. But it is a 'wilderness' specific to the South and the Mississippi; *the* dark centre of Yoknapatawpha. Its overwhelming immensity is suggested by 'the tall and endless wall of dense November woods', 'sombre, impenetrable'—so dense that it is difficult to discern 'at what point [one] could possibly hope to enter it. . .' (GDM, 148). The very opposite of 'the open country' of other American terrains, this is both a geography and language of intense association: a poetic mapping to counter the plain textual geometries of plantation and farm. Indeed in *Go Down, Moses* wood and forest, as emblematic of this wilderness condition, are consistently invoked as part of a 'soaring and sombre solitude'. If the plantation belongs to a cash-crop and slave-owning heritage and the cleared landscape of palpable control and order so the forests in their very impenetrability are part of an archetypal alternative. They suggest a sacred condition borne out of density and darkness.

Faulkner, of course, is not the first to note this sense of density in Southern forests around the Mississippi region. In *Life on the Mississippi* Twain spoke of 'dense forests which extended for miles without farm, woodyard, clearing, or break of any kind' which formed 'dim forest walls'. Similarly the Mississippi offered to the eye a 'dense, untouched forest' which, between Cairo and Baton Rouge was a 'thousand-mile wall of dense forest that guards the two banks all the way. . .'.[10] A kindred sense of magnitude made William Bartram feel himself to be 'under the shadow of a grand forest'.[11] Time and again in *Go Down, Moses*, the forests make themselves felt as part of an enveloping darkness—the condition to which Faulkner's text moves and *the* centre of an original state to counter the territorial expansion of white power, a darkness which offers an image of an inner self beyond language. At such a point, Faulkner's language becomes a rich text of suggestion and echo; his sentences so thick with multiple clauses that they achieve a weight and density equivalent to the very forests he describes.

3

If the forest offers Faulkner one of the primary icons of significance for the condition he seeks to enter and regain, against the grain of a cursed and rapacious progressive decimation of the wilderness, so the river Mississippi offers the other. In *Go Down, Moses* it emerges as the great source of power within the text—a presence given added substance in the way that the penultimate story, 'Delta Autumn', holds such a central place within the cycle of stories. Although, like 'The Bear', 'Delta Autumn' is ostensibly a hunting story based upon an older and sadder McCaslin who openly decries the continuing disappearance of the forests, it brings the river into focus to the extent that it insists on the delta lands as basic to the whole perspective of the text. Whereas in 'The Bear' McCaslin enters the forest, so in 'Delta Autumn' the annual ritual of the hunt is associated with the act of 'enter[ing] the Delta'. The effect is to suggest both a region in which to hunt, but also an entry into the ground—the soil deposited over the flood plain by the river. As the hunters travel towards the retreating forests on the delta, so Faulkner celebrates a dying ritual as their movement uncovers the text's (and the land's) great image of fertility:

> It had been renewed like this each last week in November for more than fifty years—the last hill, at the foot of which the rich unbroken alluvial flatness began as the sea began at the base of its cliffs, dissolving away beneath the unhurried November rain as the sea itself would dissolve away. (GDM, 252)

Part of the ritual of *Go Down, Moses* is that of initiation—into a condition which speaks to a primary state of being which is most obviously suggested to Faulkner by the impenetrable wilderness forests. But the foundation of this 'knowledge' is downwards. Human activity, at least that part associated with progressive and possessive expansionism across the land, is not only viewed as destructive but as merely surface deep. Man thus 'scratches' at the soil—leaving the shallowest of marks and texts. Beneath remains the 'real' inheritance of which words are only the visual sanction of Faulkner's blighted American mystery: a dark but rich substratum which exists as an equivalent consciousness of being. The delta, as such, is a depository: a metaphor of an alternative history and the true basis of Yoknapatawpha country.

Marking Out and Digging In: Language as Ritual

And the Mississippi river is basic to this geography of meaning, for the river extends the delta's significance as it equally underscores Faulkner's use of language. As Twain noted, the Mississippi 'is a remarkable river in this: that instead of widening toward its mouth, it grows narrower; grows narrower and deeper'.[12] But this is no 'great sewer' nor is it the channel of an America which, for Melville in *The Confidence-Man*, represented the

> all-fusing spirit of the West whose type is the Mississippi itself, which uniting the streams of the most distant and opposite zones, pours them along, helter-skelter, in one cosmopolitan and confident tide'.[13]

Rather, in *Go Down, Moses*, the river's presence suggests the very nervous system of a continent upon which that 'Western' spirit hacks and scratches. Its 2,348 miles length with a drainage basin extending over some 1,255,000 square miles taking in such major tributaries as the rivers Missouri, Arkansas, Red River, Ohio, Tennessee, and of course the Tallahatchie, make it indeed appropriate to its name, which as William Bartram reminds us means 'the great sire of rivers'.

The Mississippi delta is, thus, directly associated with a language of a rich and dark fecundity: a basin of significance against which all human activity over the area is gauged. But it is also an alternative historical condition: repository of endless flood waters which deposit the mud of the continent's body. The delta becomes the image of a slow but endless process, the waters of the Mississippi involved in an endless activity of acretion and secretion: an osmosis akin to Faulkner's way with words. It has, thus, a symbolic ambiguity as far from the 'imagism' of Thoreau, Pound and William Carlos Williams as one can get. Faulkner creates a sense of linguistic density mirrored in a river whose slow-moving course meanders and alters direction in its constant negotiation with the land. Its levees, bayous and ox-bows run counter to the hard-edged and straightlined geometries of man's activities. The delta is thus a point of origin and of release: not a Pacific Ocean, nor a Walden Pond, but a fecund and obscure sanctum in which the entire significance of the river, and its plain, is given absolute focus:

> The twin banks marched with wilderness as he remembered it. . . . There was some of it left, although now it was two hundred miles from Jefferson when once it had been thirty. He had watched it, not being conquered, destroyed, so much as retreating since its purpose was served now and its time an outmoded time, retreating southward through this inverted-apex, this Δ-shaped section of earth between hills and river until what was left of it seemed now to be gathered and for the time arrested in one tremendous destiny of brooding and inscrutable inpenetrability at the ultimate funnelling tip. (GDM, 259)

Once again this is the 'tip' not of a green land but of a dark and secret other—most obviously recognizable in the black waters of Edgar Allan Poe's interior landscapes.

It is against this 'brooding and inscrutable impenetrability', then, that *Go Down, Moses* laments both Southern—and American—man's guilt and corruption, and the destruction of the wilderness. Man's way with the land becomes the extension of an interior state itself the reflection of the larger values of the culture. Thus the marks on the land exist as opposing texts of recognition and significance: lexicons of distinct states of being. Against the 'ancient pathway of bear and deer' is set the vicious and abstracting energies of a segmenting geometry: 'ruthless mile-wide parallelograms wrought by ditching the dyking machinery.' The land is now 'warped and wrung to mathematical squares of rank cotton' as it retreats 'year by year before the onslaught of axe and . . . dynamite and tractor ploughs. . .'. What is called the signature of man's 'crime and guilt'.

The wilderness, delta and river thus suggest a triptych of significance whereby Faulkner seeks his icons of meaning: the base for a language appropriate to his metaphysic. In this sense guilt and corruption remain part of a fundamental condition which is as much inculcated in the land as in what is done to it. If the darkness in this wilderness area is fecund, it is also part of a frightening condition of the unknown and unspeakable: closer to that symbolic blackness of Melville and Poe than the idea of a pure America of radiance and transcendence to which Emerson and Whitman looked.

Marking Out and Digging In: Language as Ritual

Thus this 'other' which Faulkner articulates is, finally, offered in a language of silence—as inscrutable as the wilderness with which it is associated. Indeed, it is at the centre of the ageing McCaslin's epiphany towards the end of 'Delta Autumn':

> He lay on his back, his eyes closed, his breathing quiet and peaceful as a child's, listening to it—that silence which was never silence but was myriad. He could almost see it, tremendous, primeval, looming, musing downward upon this puny evanescent clutter of human sojourn. . . . (GDM, 267)

How significant, then, that in 1941 another figure associated with a Southern tradition, and a major influence on the Fugitive poets who was as distrustful of Emerson's 'Northern' spirit as is Faulkner's text, should publish his own poem to the power of the Mississippi: T. S. Eliot's 'The Dry Salvages', Part Three of *Four Quartets*. For Eliot's poem, while grounded in a Christian dogma, like Faulkner's stories, speaks to silence and inscrutability. The poem articulates a language of loneliness and ambiguity based on Eliot's own sense of a 'modern' condition. If the poem invokes 'the life of significant soil', it does so in relation to Eliot's own childhood in St. Louis and his memories of the Mississippi river. Thus the Mississippi is a 'strong brown god—sullen, untamed and intractable'. But, as in Faulkner, 'the brown god is almost forgotten/By the dwellers in cities.' The river is thus an image of a larger state: a basic consciousness which fractures the confidence of a linear and progressive view of human, and in particular American, settlement. To return to the river is akin to that silence McCaslin discovers; a return, and 'backward look behind the assurance/of recorded history, the backward half-look/over the shoulder, towards the primitive terror'.[14] *Go Down, Moses* is likewise full of 'recorded history' written on 'yellowed pages' with 'brown thin ink', just as it is full of man's calculations upon the land. But its essential perspective posits the ground itself as the primary source of meaning into which all activity comes to rest: a silence and terror which contains 'the anonymous communal original dust'.

Like Eliot, Faulkner's significant language rests in the impenetrable and unknowable: an ambiguous presence which will not be spoken. In his view of the wilderness he inscribes a needful lexicon which approaches the land's inscrutability: a poetic rendering vested in paradox, darkness and mystery. His words are thus akin to those paw-prints left by Old Ben: a 'print' in a 'markless wilderness', but, once again, neither direct nor clear-cut. The enigma McCaslin stalks leaves a 'crooked print', a 'warped indentation in the wet ground'.

Faulkner's text seeks a language equivalent to that 'indentation'. In a culture shown to be cursed and alienated, he seeks a redeeming language held amidst a dark 'other'. Like the paw-print it is a language enveloped in a 'seepage of water' but a presence which gives to the geometries of emptiness a recovered foundation based in darkness. Thus *Go Down, Moses*, while it stalks a Southern history, cuts through a social detritus down towards a bedrock of meaning: a poetic stillness of significant presence akin to Poe and Eliot. In *As I Lay Dying* Addie Bundren's voice is heard from the absence and emptiness of a home-made coffin. Her 'self', as it were, has become defined and framed by a shape, by that of the coffin. Inside, like her spirit in life, her body putrifies and rots: a composite image of a thwarted and corrupt culture defined by its hard-edged geometries. In this condition 'words are no good', no more than 'a shape to fill a lack'. And yet Annie's isolation speaks directly to a 'dark voicelessness', the 'dark land talking the voiceless speech'. This is the silence McCaslin hears as he 'lay on his back'—not in a 'coffin' certainly but *on* the land: as close to it as he could be in life. He incarnates its very spirit—waiting to be heard and recovered.

Against the general condition of displacement and loss, of power and misery pictured in *Go Down, Moses,* Faulkner seeks a true *base* for American meaning. But *Go Down, Moses* does not offer a language of escape, but of return and ritual—to an impossible point of origin—voiceless but 'there' in the ground. How appropriate, then, that the final story, 'Go Down, Moses', concerns not McCaslin but the Southern 'negro', wholly dispossessed and without property. For just as *Go Down, Moses* is dedicated to an ex-slave, so it ends with the ritual return of a Southern black to the ground of his lost inheritance. Samuel Beauchamp, displaced

Marking Out and Digging In: Language as Ritual

north and executed for murder, is brought back for burial: a ritual return home. And yet, importantly, he does not return to the surface of the land—for this is the site of his alienation—he returns *into* the soil, into the hub of the delta.

In the closing pages of the text Beauchamp's funeral is described in terms basic to the white people's way with the land. Once more we are given a language of control and direction based on train, road and car: energies, objects and directions emblematic of the geometries of fence and order strewn across the land. The linear movement of the funeral procession passes beyond this 'map'. Beauchamp's body moves over a landscape of the linear and the horizontal, without resonance or meaning, gesture or ritual. As it does so it moves elsewhere, to that condition of silence in the ground heard by McCaslin. As the body is driven along 'the country road leading to the destination seventeen miles away', so *Go Down, Moses* begins its re-entry to the wilderness through a symbolic movement downwards. Road, railway and fence are thus part of a surface text—shapes that 'fill a lack' and are reflective of the culture they image.[15] In contrast Beauchamp returns to the land itself: his body *into* the body of the continent. Not, as it were, a burial, but a homecoming, and a release, a letting-go, into the ground and significant silence. Go down, Moses, go *down*.

NOTES

1. 'Mississippi' from *Essays, Speeches and Public Letters* by William Faulkner, ed. James B. Meriwether (London: Chatto and Windus, 1967), p. 11. The whole 'essay' is of significance and recounts the disappearance of *one* South as it is replaced by another.
2. For the whole text see the version printed in *The Black Poets*, ed. Dudley Randall (New York: Bantam, 1971), p. 23. See also 'Deep River', p. 26.
3. *William Faulkner: Three Decades of Criticism*, ed. and intro. Frederick J. Hoffman and Olga W. Vickery (New York: Harcourt, Brace, Jovanovich Inc., 1960), p. 94. For Cowley in *Go Down, Moses*, 'Faulkner's theme is the negroes'.
4. Michael Millgate, *The Achievement of William Faulkner* (London: Constable, 1966), p. 202.

5. Ibid., p. 201.
6. *As I Lay Dying* (New York: Vintage Books, 1964), p. 167. The whole of Addie's 'soliloquy' is of significance.
7. *Go Down, Moses* (Harmondsworth: Penguin Books, 1960), p. 199. All subsequent references to the text appear in parentheses within the essay, prefixed by GDM.
8. *William Faulkner: Three Decades of Criticism*, p. 126. The original essay 'Wilderness and Civilization: A Note on William Faulkner' appeared in the *Partisan Review* (Summer 1955), 340–50.
9. Ibid., p. 132. See in relation to this pp. 45–55 of Yi-fu Tuan's *Landscapes of Fear* (Oxford: Basil Blackwell, 1980).
10. Mark Twain, *Life on the Mississippi* (New York: New American Library, 1961), pp. 186, 76.
11. *The Travels of William Bartrum* (New York: Dover, 1955), p. 340.
12. *Life on the Mississippi*, p. 13.
13. *The Confidence-Man* (New York: New American Library, 1964), p. 15. The whole of Chapters 1 and 2 are relevant.
14. T. S. Eliot, *Collected Poems 1909–1962* (London: Faber and Faber, 1963), p. 209.
15. Faulkner's 'map' of Jefferson, Yoknapatawpha County (reproduced in the 1951 Modern Library edition of *Absalom Absalom!*) offers a visual representation of this contrast—as basic to *Go Down, Moses* as it is to all of the Yoknapatawpha novels. The map is divided into quarters by straight roads and further sub-divided into triangular areas. Running parallel to the 'main road' (between 'Memphis Junction' and 'Mottstown') is the 'John Sartoris Railroad'—a double axis of separation as both lines literally *split* the land in two. Over this map of separation is noted incidents from the novels—narrative histories inscribed like marks onto the surface of the land. And yet there is a second 'map' which runs counter to this geometry of white order. The '2,400 square miles' of Yoknapatawpha are bounded by two rivers, the Tallahatchie at the top and the Yoknapatawpha at the bottom. Like the Mississippi they bend and curve, endlessly *turning* as part of an alternative geometry and imagery. In turn their presence is given added significance by the 'hatching' representing hills and 'natural' undulations on the land. We are given a visual representation of precisely the conflict central to *Go Down, Moses*. The final story, as it were, moves *downwards* towards the Yoknapatawpha river: beneath and away from white control, into the hub, and foundation, of the delta.

7
The Snopes Trilogy

by ANDREW HOOK

Let me begin with cards clearly on the table. I share the conventional view that the so-called Snopes trilogy—*The Hamlet* (1940), *The Town* (1957), *The Mansion* (1959)—is not one of Faulkner's very greatest achievements. Fine as they are in their different ways, these novels, unlike say *The Sound and the Fury*, *Light in August*, or *Absalom, Absalom!*, are not among the great novels of the twentieth century. Then, equally conventionally, I find *The Hamlet* easily the best of the trilogy novels. And lastly, I go along with those who find the story of Mink Snopes easily the finest thing in *The Mansion*. Given this degree of unexceptionality of critical judgment, what I propose to do in the first part of this essay is try to think around the various dimensions of the three novels so as to indicate how such judgments are ultimately arrived at.

More recent work has not succeeded in displacing Edmund Volpe's seminal assessment of the Snopes trilogy in *A Reader's Guide to William Faulkner*. Volpe's account is full of telling observations, but at this stage I want to draw attention only to one:

> Faulkner's masterpieces are great artistic creations because they create an overwhelming emotional current—despair, or pity, or outrage, or incredulity, or indignation, or horror—that tears the reader from his familiar moorings and sweeps him into a world created, shaped, and illuminated by Faulkner's personal vision of life.[1]

I am not wholly convinced that Faulkner's 'personal vision of life' has to be involved, but otherwise I find this passage profoundly true. It explains the particular quality of *intensity* that seems to me to be totally characteristic of Faulkner's writing at its best. And it is precisely its possession of this quality of intensity that marks *The Hamlet* off from *The Town* and most of *The Mansion*, and thus aligns the earlier book with the great works of Faulkner's first and most creative period. As well as intensity, however, *The Hamlet* creates a world of apparent stasis or permanence; Frenchman's Bend and the countryside surrounding it seem to be part of a permanent, unchanging, rural Southern world which Faulkner creates with a masterly vividness and immediacy:

> The team, the buckboard, went on in the thick dust of the spent summer. Now he could see the village proper—the store, the blacksmith shop, the metal roof of the gin with a thin rapid shimmer of exhaust above the stack. It was now the third week in September; the dry, dust-laden air vibrated steadily to the rapid beat of the engine, though so close were the steam and the air in temperature that no exhaust was visible but merely a thin feverish shimmer of mirage. The very hot, vivid air, which seemed to be filled with the slow laborious plaint of laden wagons, smelled of lint; wisps of it clung among the dust-stiffened roadside weeds and small gouts of cotton lay imprinted by hoof- and wheel-marks into the trodden dust. He could see the wagons too, the long motionless line of them behind the patient, droop-headed mules, waiting to advance a wagon-length at a time. . . .[2]

The sensuous effectiveness of this appears almost casual, effortless: a relaxed, vivid presence, like that of the group of men in their faded denim shirts and jeans whittling on the verandah of the Varner store. The step from this static, permanent, almost timeless rural scene into the world of legend and myth is a short one; this is how Faulkner is able to allow some of his characters—Eula, Flem, Ike—and the events in which they are involved, to acquire something of the quality of archetypal myths. From the very beginning of his career, Faulkner seems to have taken on board Eliot's advice to his contemporaries to adopt Joyce's method of using myth as a way of giving significance to 'the immense panorama of futility and anarchy which is contemporary history'.[3] In *The*

The Snopes Trilogy

Hamlet, so firmly anchored in the vividly recreated landscapes and settings of the rural South, the method is still at work, enlarging and universalizing the meaning of the minute particulars of character and event. Flem Snopes appears first in the novel as a face at a window. Then this:

> One moment the road had been empty, the next moment the man stood there beside it, at the edge of a small copse—the same cloth cap, the same rhythmically chewing jaw materialised apparently out of nothing and almost abreast of the horse, with an air of the completely and purely accidental which Varner was to remember and speculate about only later. (pp. 20–1)

Flem seems, as it were, to materialize out of nowhere; he is simply a presence—and that is what he remains from the beginning of *The Hamlet* to the end of *The Mansion*.

Volpe speaks of the 'tonal and thematic contrasts' that shape and structure the meaning of *The Hamlet* given the fact that Flem remains an absent presence for most of the novel.[4] More basic still, perhaps, is the contrast between the slow, unhurried, almost static world of the novel and the amazing intensity of action and feeling in the stories it contains. The two elements play off against each other in a manner that heightens both, and contributes significantly to that 'unmooring' of the reader's familiar sense of reality to which Volpe refers. Ultimately, however, Faulkner's fictional reality is a creation of his language and style. In all of his best work language and style seem to set aside referential reality; the reader has to repossess, re-read the world. Rather than describing reality, Faulkner's rhetoric constantly creates or recreates it. It exists only in and through the words; rich and detailed, it is nonetheless independent, suspended, beyond time and space. Conventional grammar and syntax are often sacrificed to allow the emergence of this new world in which past and present, the immediate and the mythical, the static and the transient, flow in and out of each other. In the case of *The Hamlet*, style lends additional intensity to the given intensity of action, event and feeling:

> The moon was almost full then. When supper was over and they had gathered again along the veranda, the alteration was

hardly one of visibility even. It was merely a translation from the lapidary-dimensional of day to the treacherous and silver receptivity in which the horses huddled in mazy camouflage, or singly or in pairs rushed, fluid, phantom, and unceasing, to huddle again in mirage-like clumps from which came high abrupt squeals and the vicious thudding of hooves. (pp. 247–48)

The ponies described here are extra-ordinary, praeternatural, the moonlight simply reinforcing their larger-than-life, almost surreal existence. But the particular effects of such a descriptive passage in fact mirror the essential characteristics of the stories that *The Hamlet* tells: Flem Snopes's rapacious acquisitiveness; Eula's sexuality; Labove's passion; Mink Snopes's fury; Armstid's treasure lust; Ike's love for his cow; Lump Snopes's greed. All of these, as well as a whole series of inset life-stories, episodes, or incidents, are characterized by the same sense of a driving intensity of felt experience. The Snopes establish themselves in Yoknapatawpha County by actual and threatened barn-burning. But flames and fire are appropriate metaphors for the all-consuming passions that seem to possess and drive so many of the characters in *The Hamlet*, and are communicated to the reader by a constantly and cumulatively creative language and style.

It is the general absence of any comparable passionate intensity that explains the relative inferiority of *The Town* and *The Mansion*. For long stretches of both these novels a kind of relaxed, meditative rumination replaces intensity. Perhaps on occasion Gavin Stevens's mental agonizing's attain a kind of intensity of their own, but it is still an inadequate substitute. Indeed, the use of Stevens as a narrator—along with Charles Mallison and V. K. Ratliff—is the obvious source of the problem. Stevens is both character and narrator in both novels, and his personality seems to set the tone of both works. Stevens may or may not be a Faulkner mouthpiece—the truth probably is that sometimes he is, sometimes he is not. But as Harvard graduate, Heidelberg Ph.D., lawyer, humanist and romantic idealist, he has little in common with the driven characters of *The Hamlet*. Of course he is caught up in the events he describes, and he has passions and feelings of his own, but there is simultaneously a quality of intellectual

The Snopes Trilogy

detachment about him; he is a tolerant, liberal observer of the complexities of life. Thus he—and his fellow narrators—work to distance the reader from the events they describe, keeping the imaginative pressure at a noticeably lower level. Faulkner himself was quite aware of the change: 'Doing a little work on the next Snopes book,' he wrote to Saxe Commins, 'have not taken fire in the old way yet, so it goes slow. . . .'[5] About the same time he wrote to his young friend Jean Stein seeking reassurance over the Snopes material he had sent her:

> I still feel, as I did last year, that perhaps I have written myself out and all that remains now is the empty craftsmanship—no fire, force, passion anymore in the words and sentences.[6]

For me at least, this is more or less accurate. What one misses above all in *The Town*—and in much of *The Mansion* too—is just these particular qualities at the level of language and style, words and sentences. Faulkner was in no sense written out; but his stance towards his material had changed in the direction suggested by his readiness to employ Gavin Stevens as his principal narrator.

Seventeen years separate *The Hamlet* and *The Town*, and of course there is no reason why Faulkner should have attempted to re-achieve in the later novel what he had done in the earlier one. Cleanth Brooks reminds us that we do well to try to read *The Town* 'by its own light and to judge it by its own standards'.[7] (However Brooks goes on to take the somewhat extreme position of suggesting that readers of the trilogy might well be advised to omit reading *The Town* altogether and move straight from *The Hamlet* to *The Mansion*.) Again, many elements of the Snopes trilogy had been gestating for much longer than seventeen years, and Faulkner himself drew attention to this point in the prefatory note he wrote for *The Mansion*. He said he knew that there were 'discrepancies and contradictions' between different elements in the stories written at widely different times: these were due to the fact that the author had learned 'more about the human heart and its dilemma than he knew thirty-four years ago'. Faulkner implies by this that there is no reason to expect the trilogy to contain any kind of uniformity or consistency in such areas as tone, attitude, or vision. The trilogy has changed as its author has changed. Some commentators on the trilogy have indeed tried to argue that Faulkner's comment has a substantially wider significance than a simple defence of local discrepancies and contradictions.[8] Faulkner does actually mean that he has learned more about the human heart: *The Town* and *The Mansion* are the work of an older and wiser man. Specifically, in the later novels, the characters who appear in *The Hamlet* as archetypes, larger than life embodiments of primitive human passions and drives, are now scaled down to more recognizable, complex, human beings. Perhaps so. But whatever the cause, the result is a lessening of impact upon the reader. Stevens, Mallison, and Ratliff, mediating to the reader the activities of the inhabitants of *The Town* and *The Mansion*, seem to some degree to defuse their impact. Faulkner himself seems sometimes to be aware of this: he tells us that Stevens talks too much. In *The Town* he allows Ratliff to observe of Stevens: 'You never listened to nobody because by that time you were already talking again.'[9] Not that Ratliff's judgment compares in severity with that of young Charles Mallison made, not in the trilogy, but in *Knight's Gambit*:

> What surprised him was his uncle: that glib and talkative man who talked so much and so glibly, particularly about things which had absolutely no concern with him, that his was indeed a split personality: the one, the lawyer, the county attorney who walked and breathed and displaced air; the other, the garrulous facile voice so garrulous and facile that it seemed to have no connection with reality at all and presently hearing it was like listening not even to fiction but to literature.[10]

But such acid comments by his fellow-narrators have little effect on that aspect of Faulkner which seems to coincide with Stevens's wordiness, and Stevens remains the dominating voice in both *The Town* and *The Mansion*. Of course not all commentators are quite so critical of Stevens. It is Warren Beck, in *Man in Motion*, who has written easily the most elaborate account of the Snopes trilogy. Throughout his book, Beck argues for the coherence, consistency and sustained imaginative achievement of all three novels; one can only agree with Cleanth Brooks that anyone seriously concerned with the trilogy must consult such a sensitive and intelligent book. Hence when Beck makes the following observation on those of us who see the Mink Snopes story in *The Mansion* as easily the most brilliant and compelling thing in the two later novels, one is bound to pay attention:

> ... those who praise the Mink Snopes portion as though it were self-sustained and extractable are perhaps only failing to sense how much their response draws on the rest of the trilogy, through a reader's marginal consciousness of the relevant, and particularly as to the tangential illumination projected across the action by Stevens, Ratliff, and Charles.[11]

Beck may very well be right. But one cannot help noticing that none of these three narrators tell the story of Mink. Instead Faulkner reverts to the anonymous, authorial narrative voice which had appeared throughout most of *The Hamlet*. I would argue that it is only thus that Faulkner could have achieved the remarkable feat of bringing the reader over to Mink's murderous side.

Brooks is right to suggest that Faulkner does not make it easy for us to admire Mink Snopes.[12] In *The Town* Ratliff calls him 'the only out-and-out mean Snopes we ever experienced' (p. 71); and the murder of Houston in *The Hamlet* is an outrageous act unredeemed even by its inevitability. The murder of Houston does not surprise us; it is at one with the urgent, unyielding intensity of Mink's savage stubbornness, perseverance, and driving desperation. If the gun had not exploded, he, we feel, would have done. Given this pitching of Mink beyond any normal pitch of intensity, inevitably there are suggestions of the transformation of the poor, down-trodden, struggling dirt-farmer, into someone epic, even heroic. Nonetheless, after the murderous ambush of Houston, another driven man, the reader's sympathy is more with Houston's indomitable and faithful hound, refusing, despite Mink's repeated assaults, to abandon its dead master, than with Mink himself. Yet in the subsequent episodes, despite this background, Faulkner reverses the situation.

Denied help of any kind by Flem, Mink is sent to Parchman jail in 1908; manoeuvred by Flem into a futile attempt to escape, he is caught and resentenced in 1923; finally pardoned he leaves Parchman in 1946 having served thirty-eight years. His one surviving aim is to kill the kinsman who has betrayed him. In the course of the brilliant narrative account of how he does it, Mink re-emerges as a character of heroic and epic proportions. Just as Dickens achieves a powerful imaginative identity with the hunted Bill Sikes after the murder of Nancy, so Faulkner compels us into sharing Mink's unswerving conviction of the absolute necessity of his doing what he has set out to do. Mink's intensity is transferred hypnotically to the reader; his concerns—over the unfamiliar world he finds himself in after the long years in Parchman, over his tiny hoard of dollars, over the ancient pistol and cartridges he buys, over 'Old Moster's' sense of justice—echo increasingly as our own. Stevens and the other narrators become involved in Mink's story; but the narrative itself remains independent of them, and perhaps that is its strength.

Late in *The Town*, Charles Mallison, the youngest of the three narrators, has an exchange with Ratliff about the use or non-use of Southern vernacular forms of speech. The point at issue is the use of 'drug' for standard English 'dragged'. Charles objects to Ratliff's use of the standard word, arguing that the vernacular form has a greater potency: ' "drug" sounds a heap more dragged than just "dragged".' However Ratliff retorts that for ten years he has been trying 'to say words right'; he has had the same argument with Charles's uncle who ended up saying 'ain't I got as much right to use your *drug* for my *dragged* as you got to use my *dragged* for your *drug*?' (p. 236). Without making too much of this minor, if somewhat odd, exchange, one might argue that it hints at some degree of ambivalence on Faulkner's own part over issues that include but go beyond the question of the kind of language in which *The Town* and *The Mansion* is written.[13]

The Hamlet is a wholly Yoknapatawpha County novel. *The Town* and *The Mansion* are Yoknapatawpha novels only to a limited degree. The link between Yoknapatawpha and the

The Snopes Trilogy

blossoming of Faulkner's creative genius is beyond dispute; from the point of view of imaginative creativity he himself insisted on the central value of his 'own little postage stamp of native soil' as a kind of inexhaustible 'gold mine' which he could go on exploiting.[14] Of course the Jefferson of *The Town* and *The Mansion* is part of Yoknapatawpha, but the felt experience for the reader is somehow very different. It is all more up-to-date. V. K. Ratliff's use of 'drug'—not to mention Stevens's—is in danger of seeming merely quaint, a touch of local colour. This seems to me to point to the larger problem. Faulkner's brooding genius seems to have required a sense of the South and Southern history for its fullest articulation. The minute particulars of Yoknapatawpha County, which lend such a tangible, sensuous reality to the scenes and settings and landscapes, the contexts and characters of Faulkner's major narratives, all seem to belong to an older, unchanging, Southern world. Conspicuously absent from this world is any sense of *contemporary* America. *The Town* and in particular *The Mansion* are very much a different matter. Gavin Stevens and Charles Mallison belong to a world in which 'dragged' has supplanted 'drug'. The action of *The Town* goes back to the period before World War I and goes on into the 1920s; *The Mansion* covers the period of the 1930s and 1940s. More important is the way in which action and characters are caught up—at least to some degree—in the major, external historical events of these decades. Thus the novels contain comment on public events to a degree that is noticeably greater than is the case in the fiction of Faulkner's great period. Why this matters is that, in my view, Faulkner and his narrators rarely have especially compelling things to say about the contemporary modern world. Perhaps Volpe is correct when he suggests that the problem is 'Faulkner's emotional detachment from his material'.[15] Certainly there is a qualitative difference between Faulkner's references to, say, the Spanish Civil War, and the American Civil War. Faulkner knows about the former but is possessed by the latter: the result is writing of very different degrees of intensity.

Perhaps the underlying point is Faulkner's familiar conviction that there is no such thing as the past:

> There is no such thing really as was because the past is. It is a part of every man, every woman, and every moment. All of his and her ancestry, background, is all a part of himself and herself at any moment.[16]

Just this metaphysic of time is of course built in to all of Faulkner's fiction. Over and over again he insists on and dramatizes the notion that the past is never over; that both present and future are contained in the past; that the present is only the confirmation of what has already happened. Even his style, or at least one aspect of his style—the long, winding, ungrammatical sentences—appears to be a rhetorical articulation of such a metaphysic: within the single unfolding sentence past, present and future hang compacted and suspended.

When he was writing the Snopes trilogy Faulkner clearly felt about the nature of time just as he had always done. But in *The Town* and *The Mansion* the interweaving of past and present, the retelling of the past in the present, the present's confirmation of what was always going to happen—these phenomena have gained a somewhat mechanical air. And contemporary history itself is no more than that: a given backdrop against which present events are foregrounded. Faulkner's profounder sense of history, of the past's continuing presence, now operates to a major degree only within the history of his own creative life as a writer. What any analysis of the writing history of the Snopes trilogy reveals is the astonishing degree to which it represents a rewriting of Faulkner's own writing history. The origins of the Snopes as a potential subject for Faulkner lie back in the early 1920s at the very start of his writing career. In a very real sense he never stopped writing about the Snopes throughout his entire writing life.

Of course Faulkner's readiness to rework and re-deploy existing material is a constant factor in his writing practice. But nowhere is this readiness carried so far as in the case of the Snopes trilogy. *The Hamlet* involves the revising and retelling of five existing, published stories; *The Town* incorporates two more existing stories; and *The Mansion* two more again. Then *The Town* retells a great deal of what had occurred in *The Hamlet*, while *The Mansion*

The Snopes Trilogy

involves still further recapitulation: stories already told are told again. Faulkner always insisted that the four sections of *The Sound and the Fury* were four attempts to tell the same story, and that the Introduction he wrote for the Modern Library edition was a fifth attempt. The same principle is at work in the Snopes trilogy producing in some instances the well known discrepancies in the different accounts of the same events which so worried Faulkner's original editors. The author himself did not regard these lapses as very important. In a letter written while he was working on *The Mansion*, he insisted that his characters were for him 'quite real and quite constant'; he may sometimes forget what they did,

> but the character I don't forget, and when the book is finished, that character is not done, he still is going on at some new devilment that sooner or later I will find out about and write about.[17]

In other words, like the past, a character is never over. As John E. Basset puts it, in *The Mansion* the theme of the return to the past 'becomes Faulkner's method: conscious revision of earlier material in a process of both recapitulation and transformation'.[18] Hence at the end of the day there is no closure to Faulkner's fiction; here in the Snopes trilogy even his method of composition can be seen as another enactment of the view inherent in his employment of a variety of narrator figures each one commenting on the other and on the events and characters they describe. Finally there can be no single, true story: the same story can be told and retold by one voice or several. No one version is ever the final version.

That Faulkner's method as creator and narrator so resists closure should warn us not to look for the absolutes of moral judgments in the content of his fiction. Hence it is surprising to discover that some of the most hotly debated critical issues in the Snopes trilogy focus on questions of moral judgment. Most commentators agree that throughout the trilogy V. K. Ratliff is a sympathetic figure. A major opponent of Snopesism, in the course of the trilogy he wins some battles even if he loses others. As a narrator he seems to emerge from the American Western tall-tale tradition; one feels that Ratliff and Mark Twain would have got along pretty well. But of course Ratliff is an active participant in the affairs of Yoknapatawpha County, not just a sidelines narrator. Hence questions about his behaviour may well arise. Presumably most readers approve of Ratliff's manoeuvrings over Mink's sewing-machine and the goats which lead to Flem's at least partial defeat early in *The Hamlet*; equally, though a shade or two less persuasively, we accept that his falling for the salted mine trick later on in *The Hamlet* reveals his sharing in the weaknesses of ordinary humanity. It is his behaviour in another episode that has been seen as giving rise to a moral problem.

A central concern of 'The Long Summer' section of *The Hamlet* is Ike Snopes's love for a cow. For the idiot Ike the cow is a love-object with all the grandeur and beauty of the most legendary and fabulous females in world history. Given his cow by Houston, Ike and his beloved become a money-spinning peepshow for Lump Snopes. Ratliff puts an end to the affair. It is this intervention that has sparked critical argument. Some commentators rebuke Ratliff for allowing conventional notions of moral decorum to take precedence over human concern for the pitiful Ike: Ratliff's outrage, it is argued, is destructive of Ike's love.[19] Ike's love is pure and harmless; it is a positive in the bleak, self-seeking world of Frenchman's Bend. But Ratliff chooses to wipe it out.

Now it is true that Ratliff himself is less than certain that his actions and motives are beyond reproach:

> 'I aint never disputed I'm a pharisee,' he said. 'You dont need to tell me he aint got nothing else. I know that. Or that I can sholy leave him have at least this much. I know that too. Or that besides, it aint any of my business. I know that too, just as I know that the reason I aint going to leave him have what he does have is simply because I am strong enough to keep him from it. I am stronger that him. Not righter. Not any better, maybe. But just stronger.'[20]

Nonetheless, I am not inclined to think that this is an issue on which Faulkner invites the reader to pass judgment—either for or against Ratliff. Quite fundamental to Faulkner's fiction is the absence of authorial intervention

The Snopes Trilogy

for moral or any other reasons. It is something of a cliché to suggest that great writers allow their characters independent life; in Faulkner's case the cliché contains a large measure of truth. His letter on the characters in *The Mansion*, quoted above, may strike some readers as either naïve or precious; but his practice goes a long way towards authenticating the implied position. Faulkner's characters are exactly men—or women—in motion; they take possession of the stories in which they are involved; driven, doomed, or whatever, they seem simply to be themselves, doing whatever they are compelled to do. Ratliff being Ratliff intervenes as he does; the rightness or wrongness of the intervention, except in so far as he himself debates it, is not the issue. In conversation at the University of Virginia, Faulkner said: 'Maybe the writer has no concept of morality at all, only an integrity to hold always to what he believes to be the facts and truths of human behaviour.'[21] Not, I agree once again, that there is anything very exceptional about such a view; most modernist writers, at least, would subscribe to it. Certainly in Faulkner's case there is never any question of a rush to judgment; we may not admire what Flem Snopes does, but to condemn him as bad or evil hardly seems relevant. Certainly to arrive at such a judgment seems not to be Faulkner's reason for writing about him. One may choose to agree or disagree with Ratliff's actions over Ike and the cow, but no critical issue is in fact involved; condemnation or approval of Ratliff is not the point. 'There arent any morals', Stevens said. 'People just do the best they can.'[21] Warren Beck is probably right to argue that Stevens speaks here with his author's voice.[23]

As a final statement, an ultimate truth, such a conclusion may seem modest indeed. Nonetheless, it may be in part what Faulkner means when he insists in the note prefaced to *The Mansion* that he has learned more about the human heart and its dilemma than he knew thirty-four years before. Certainly the statement is part of the 'poor sons of bitches' motif which most commentators agree seems to sum up Faulkner's sense of the human condition at the end of the Snopes trilogy. We may recall that 'the poor son-of-a-bitch' is Owl-eyes' epitaph upon Jay Gatsby at the end of Fitzgerald's novel; but Nick Carraway invites the reader to see some larger meaning in Gatsby's fate. The Snopes trilogy offers no such larger meaning. Only the splendid poetry of Gavin Stevens, near the end of *The Town*, looking down in 'the dying last of day' watching the fireflies 'myriad and frenetic, random and frantic, pulsing; not questing, not quiring, but choiring as if they were tiny incessant appeaseless voices, cries, words', looking down upon the whole world of Yoknapatawpha County, creating in firefly words 'this miniature of man's passions and hopes and disasters—ambition and fear and lust and courage and abnegation and pity and honour and sin and pride' (p. 271). Or the equally blazing final paragraph of *The Mansion* recording Mink Snopes's absorption into the earth:

> the ground already full of the folks that had the trouble but were free now, so that it was just the ground and the dirt that had to bother and worry and anguish with the passions and hopes and skeers, the justice and the injustice and the griefs, leaving the folks themselves easy now, all mixed and jumbled up comfortable and easy so wouldn't nobody even know or even care who was which any more, himself among them, equal to any, good as any, brave as any, being inextricable from, anonymous with all of them: the beautiful, the splendid, the proud and the brave, right on up to the very top itself among the shining phantoms and dreams which are the milestones of the long human recording—Helen and the bishops, the kings and the unhomed angels, the scornful and graceless seraphim. (p. 398)

No larger meaning perhaps; but life is permanently enriched by Faulkner's art.

NOTES

1. Edmund Volpe, *A Reader's Guide to William Faulkner* (London: Thames and Hudson, 1964), p. 330.
2. William Faulkner, *The Hamlet* (London: Chatto and Windus, 1957), p. 150. All subsequent page references are to this edition.
3. See T. S. Eliot, 'Ulysses, Order and Myth', *The Dial* (November, 1923), 480–83.
4. Volpe, *op. cit.*, p. 307.

The Snopes Trilogy

5. See Joseph Blotner (ed.), *Selected Letters of William Faulkner* (London: Scolar Press, 1977), p. 390. Faulkner was writing in December 1955 or January 1956.
6. *Ibid.*, p. 391.
7. Cleanth Brooks, *William Faulkner: The Yoknapatawpha Country* (New Haven and London: Yale University Press, 1963), p. 193.
8. See, for example, Woodrow Stroble, 'Flem Snopes: A Crazed Mirror' in Glenn O. Carey, Woodrow Stroble (eds.) *Faulkner: The Unappeased Imagination, A Collection of Critical Essays* (Troy, New York: Whitston Pub. Co., 1980), pp. 195–212.
9. William Faulkner, *The Town* (London: Chatto and Windus, 1958), p. 199. All subsequent references are to this edition.
10. William Faulkner, *Knight's Gambit* (London: Chatto and Windus, 1951), pp. 122–23.
11. Warren Beck, *Man in Motion: Faulkner's Trilogy* (Madison: University of Wisconsin Press, 1963), p. 130.
12. Brooks, *op. cit.*, pp. 220–21.
13. Earlier in the novel Charles Mallison tells us that while he was just City Attorney, Gavin Stevens talked 'Harvard and Heidelberg'; running for County Attorney he 'began to talk like the people . . . saying "drug" for "dragged" '. See p. 147.
14. See Joseph Blotner, *Faulkner: A Biography* (London: Chatto and Windus, 1974), Vol. I, pp. 526–27.
15. Volpe, *op. cit.* p. 330.
16. Frederick L. Gwynn and Joseph L. Blotner (eds.), *Faulkner in the University* (Charlottesville, Virginia: The University of Virginia Press, 1959), p. 84. Quoted by Beck, *op. cit.*, p. 192.
17. See Blotner, *op. cit.*, II, pp. 1657–658.
18. John E. Basset, 'Yoknapatawpha Revised: Demystifying Snopes', *College Literature*, 15 (1988), 145.
19. Both Thomas Y. Greet in 'The Theme and Structure of Faulkner's *The Hamlet*' and Joseph Gold in 'The Normality of Snopesism' adopt this position. Their essays are reprinted in Linda W. Wagner, *William Faulkner: Four Decades of Criticism* (Michigan State University Press, 1973), pp. 302–18 and 318–27. Brooks—*op. cit.*, pp. 407–10—defends Ratliff.
20. It is impossible to provide a page reference for this passage from the Chatto and Windus edition as, extraordinarily, the relevant closing section of 'The Long Summer' chapter was cut out by the English publishers.
21. *Faulkner in the University, op. cit.*, p. 267. Quoted by Beck, *op. cit.*, p. 116.
22. William Faulkner, *The Mansion* (London: Chatto and Windus, 1961), p. 392.
23. See Beck, *op. cit.*, p. 116.

Notes on Contributors

GRAHAM CLARKE is Lecturer in English and American Literature at the University of Kent. He is editor of *The American City: Literary and Cultural Perspectives* (1988) and *The New American Writing* (1990), both volumes in the Critical Studies series. Vision/St. Martin's will also publish his *Walt Whitman: The Poem as Private History* in 1990. His other recent articles have dealt with T. S. Eliot, Alfred Stieglitz and American landscape painting.

ANDREW HOOK is Bradley Professor of English Literature at the University of Glasgow. His American interests are reflected by his books *Scotland and America 1750–1835* (1975) and *American Literature in Context* (111) (1982) as well as by articles on Anglo-American relations.

JAMES H. JUSTUS, Distinguished Professor of English at Indiana University, has written on such American authors as Charles Brockden Brown, Hawthorne, Hemingway, Faulkner and other twentieth-century writers of the American South. His most recent book is *The Achievement of Robert Penn Warren* (1981).

A. ROBERT LEE is Senior Lecturer in English and American Literature at the University of Kent at Canterbury. He is editor of the Everyman *Moby-Dick* (1975) and of ten previous collections in the Critical Studies Series, among the most recent, *Edgar Allan Poe: The Design of Order* (1986), *First-Person Singular: Studies in American Autobiography* (1988), *Scott Fitzgerald: The Promises of Life* (1989) and *The Modern American Novella* (1989). He is author of a monograph *Black American Fiction Since Richard Wright* (1983) and a wide range of essays on American culture.

Notes on Contributors

ERIC MOTTRAM is Professor of English and American Literature at King's College in the University of London. He is the author of many works on nineteenth- and twentieth-century American culture, including *William Burroughs: The Algebra of Need*, *William Faulkner: A Profile*, and *The Rexroth Reader*. His most recent publications include a collection of essays, *Blood on the Nash Ambassador*, and his *Collected Poems*.

FAITH PULLIN teaches English and American literature at the University of Edinburgh. She is editor of *New Perspectives on Melville* (1978) and has published essays on D. H. Lawrence, Afro-American literature, Hemingway, Faulkner and Muriel Spark. She is currently completing a book on *Women Modernist Writers*. She is a book-reviewer for the *Times Higher Educational Supplement* and *Times Literary Supplement*.

DAVID TIMMS is Lecturer in American Literature at the University of Manchester. He has written on contemporary British poetry, and on British and American literature of the nineteenth and twentieth centuries. He recently published *Nathaniel Hawthorne* in the pamphlet series of the British Association for American Studies.

Index

Aaron, Daniel, 28
Adams, Henry, 114
Agee, James, and Evans, Walker: *Let Us Now Praise Famous Men*, 136
Anderson, Sherwood, 10, 11, 45, 65, 100

Bachelard, Gaston, 28
Bakhtin, Mikhail, 18, 130, 131, 133, 134, 142, 144
Balzac, Honoré de, 97
Barthes, Roland, 55
Bartram, William, 157, 159
Baudelaire, Charles, 45
Beardsley, Aubrey, 22, 28, 45
Beauvoir, Simone de, 45
Beck, Warren, 170, 177
Beerbohm, Max: 'A Sequelula to *The Dynasts*', 86
Berman, Louis, 65
Bingham, George Caleb, 27
Bleikasten, André, 129, 136, 142
Blotner, Joseph, 65, 79; *William Faulkner's Library*, 95
Bradford, William, 114
Brogan, Hugh, 138
Bromwich, David, 35
Brooks, Cleanth: *William Faulkner: The Yoknapatawpha Country*, 128
Brumm, Ursula, 152

Camus, Albert, 16, 45
Cash, W. J., 139; *The Mind of the South*, 17, 138
Chodorow, Nancy, 71
Civil Rights, 7, 32, 53
Coindreau, Maurice, 16
Conrad, Joseph, 10, 45, 85, 106; *Heart of Darkness*, 10; *The Secret Agent*, 49
Cooper, James Fenimore: *The Pioneers*, 154
Cowley, Malcolm, 8, 19, 21, 31, 43, 124; (ed.) *The Portable Faulkner*, 8, 22, 43, 148; *The Faulkner-Cowley File*, 124
Crèvecoeur, M. G. J. de: *Letters from an American Farmer*, 114
Cummings, E. E.: *The Enormous Room*, 103

Derrida, Jacques, 55
Dickens, Charles, 12, 44
Dos Passos, John: *The Grand Design*, 103
Dostoevsky, Fedor, 97, 131; *The Brothers Karamasov*, 104; *The Idiot*, 49
Douglas, Mary, 141, 143
Duncan, Robert, 114

Eliot, T. S., 45, 65, 114, 161, 162; *Four Quartets*, 161; 'The Waste Land', 48
Ellis, Havelock, 65
Ellison, Ralph 17
Ellman, Richard, 36
Emerson, Ralph Waldo, 12, 160; *Nature*, 149
Empson, William, 114

Falkner, Colonel John, 9
Falkner, Maud, 9
Falkner, Murray, 9
Falkner, Colonel William C.: *The White Rose of Memphis*, 9
Faulkner, Estelle, 14
Faulkner, Jill, 14
Faulkner, William—Essays: 'Kentucky: May: Saturday', 34; *Mirrors of Chartres Street*, 10; 'Mississippi', 7, 34, 147; *New Orleans Sketches*, 10, 45; *Salmagundi*, 10; Interviews: *Faulkner in the University*, 42, 46, 47, 54, 57; Novels: *A Fable*, 16, 18, 21, 101–6, 108, 117; *Absalom, Absalom!*, 13–14, 18, 22, 27, 32–3, 46, 57–61, 96, 97, 106, 148; *As I Lay Dying*, 12,

18, 25, 46, 54–7, 58, 73–4, 115–16, 148, 150, 162; *Flags in the Dust*, 29; *Intruder in the Dust*, 14, 27, 32, 38, 86, 90, 98, 110; *Knight's Gambit*, 15; *Light in August*, 13, 18, 27, 58, 66–71, 86, 116–19, 128–46, 148; *Mayday*, 29, 30; *Mosquitoes*, 10, 37, 64, 65; *Pylon*, 14, 100, 101–3; *Sanctuary*, 12–13, 14, 76–9, 87, 89, 90, 91, 115; *Sartoris*, 7, 11–12, 99, 148; Snopes Trilogy: 14, 15, 58, 80–2, 119–25, 165–79—*The Hamlet*, 14, 15, 27, 37, 58, 80, 88, 119, 120, 165–68, 176–78; *The Mansion*, 14, 17, 58, 64, 80, 86, 119, 165, 168–74, 175, 176, 177, 178; *The Town*, 9, 14, 27, 30–1, 32, 58, 80, 120, 121–23, 165, 168–70, 171–78; *Soldier's Pay*, 10, 43; *The Sound and the Fury*, 12, 18, 27, 46, 47–53, 58, 71–3, 96, 148, 154; *The Wild Palms*, 14, 25, 64, 74–6, 86, 88, 94–5, 100, 119; Play: *Requiem for a Nun*, 16, 76, 79–80, 85, 88, 90, 91; Poetry; *The Marble Faun*, 9, 28, 36, 45, 88–9; *A Green Bough*, 9, 89; Stories: 'A Courtship', 16; 'A Justice', 106, 125; 'Barn Burning', 15–16; 'Carcassonne', 29, 30; 'Delta Autumn', 16, 111, 148, 155; 'Dry September', 15; 'Go Down, Moses', 148, 162; 'Pantaloon in Black', 88, 148; 'Red Leaves', 15; 'That Evening Sun', 15; 'The Bear', 16, 95, 113–14, 148, 155–57, 158; 'The Fire and the Hearth', 111, 148; 'The Old People', 16, 106, 148; 'Was', 148, 153; Story-Collections: *Collected Stories of William Faulkner*, 15; *Go Down, Moses and Other Stories*, 15, 16, 18, 87, 110–14, 147–64; *Doctor Martino and Other Stories*, 14, 15; *The Unvanquished*, 14, 64; *These Thirteen*, 14, 15, 28, 125
Fitzgerald, Scott, 44, 100; *The Great Gatsby*, 13, 177–78
Flaubert, Gustave, 38
Fowler, Doreen, 69, 70
Freud, Sigmund, 45, 93; *Civilization and its Discontents*, 96
Full Metal Jacket, 106
Fulton, Keith Louise, 64

Grau, Shirley Ann, 17

Haas, R. K., 21
Hardy, Thomas, 12, 44, 85
Hawthorne, Nathaniel, 12, 44, 45, 56, 68; 'The Custom House', 59; *The Scarlet Letter*, 91
Hawthorne, Sophia, 37
Held, John 22
Hellström, Gustaf, 43
Hemingway, Ernest, 35, 44, 85, 105; *A Farewell to Arms*, 86, 93, 103; *For Whom the Bell Tolls*, 103
Holiday, 34
Holman, C. Hugh, 130, 143
Hoover, Herbert, 136

I'll Take my Stand, 114
Irving, Washington, 27

Jones, Anne, 78
Joyce, James, 10, 45; *Dubliners*, 10; *Ulysses*, 48
Jurgen, 22

Kazin, Alfred, 86
Keats John: 'Ode to a Grecian Urn', 95, 113
Kennedy, John F., 7
Kreiswirth, Martin, 130–34

Les Temps Modernes, 45
Lévi-Strauss, Claude, 111
Lind, Ilse Dusoir, 65
Lowell, Robert, 22

Mallarmé, Stephane, 45
Mars-Jones, Adam, 74
Masters, Edgar Lee: *Spoon River Anthology*, 21
McCabe, Colin, 131
McCullers, Carson, 17
Melville, Herman, 36, 45, 54, 97, 160; *Moby-Dick*, 48, 151, 153, 155; *The Confidence-Man*, 159
Meriwether, James B., 34, 38
Meyerhof, Hans: *The Philosophy of History in our Time*, 97
Miller, Perry: *The Life of the Mind in America*, 109
Milton, John, 27
Mississippi, University of, 9
Mitchell, Margaret: *Gone with the Wind*, 8

Index

Nietzsche, Frederick, 125
Nobel Prize, The, 16, 42, 43

Ober, Harold, 21
O'Connor, Flannery, 17
Olson, Charles: *Maximus IV*, 96

Page, Sally, 74
Paris Review, 7, 54, 71, 75, 95, 96, 97
Poe, Edgar Allan, 12, 43, 149, 150, 160, 162; 'The Fall of the House of Usher', 8, 47
Polk, Noel, 71
Pound, Ezra, 97, 159; *The Cantos*, 103
Prohibition, 138

Riley, John, 26
Rimbaud, Arthur, 45
Roosevelt, F. D., 138
Rovere, Richard, 130

Sacco and Vanzetti, 140
Sartre, Jean-Paul, 45
Shakespeare, William, 45, 97
Sherman, General William Tecumseh, 45
Simpson, Lewis B., 36
Smith, Al, 138
Sports Illustrated, 34
Spratling, William 10
Stein, Jean, 7, 71
Stevens, Wallace, 57
Stone, Phil, 9, 28

Styron, William, 17
Susman, Warren I.: *Culture as History*, 97
Swinburne, Algernon, Charles, 10, 28, 65

Tarkington, Booth, 100
Thoreau, Henry David, 12, 149, 159; *Walden*, 149
Times-Picayune, 10, 45, 89
Tuan, Yi-Fu, 28
Twain, Mark, 12; *Huckleberry Finn*, 47; *Life on the Mississippi*, 100

Verlaine, Paul, 45, 65
Virginia, University of, 17
Volpe, Edmond L., 165
Volstead Act, 138

Warren, Robert Penn, 17, 28
Welty, Eudora, 17
White, Hayden: *Metahistory*; 96
Whitman, Walt, 65, 149, 160
Williams, Tennessee: *Orpheus Descending*, 86; *Sweet Bird of Youth*, 86; *The Glass Menagerie*, 47
Williams, William Carlos, 159; *Paterson*, 149
Wright, Richard, 17

Yellow Book, The, 22, 45
Young, Stark: *So Red the Rose*, 26